A gift for:

Megan Solo

From:

DeBorah B. ☺

Happy mother's day.

LauGHinG in the
Midst of Mothering

Finding Joy in Being a Mom

Linda Ann Crosby

randall house

114 Bush Rd I Nashville, TN 37217
randallhouse.com

Laughing in the Midst of Mothering

© 2008 by Linda Ann Crosby

Published by Randall House Publications
114 Bush Road
Nashville, TN 37217

Printed in the United States of America

ISBN 10: 0892655577
ISBN 13: 9780892655571

To my mother, Grace E. Nikander,
thank you for teaching me the tricks of the trade.

To my husband, Rickey Allan Crosby,
thank you for choosing me to mother your children.

To my children, Larisa Christine, Austin Rick and
Keeve Kennedy,
thank you for providing endless writing material.
Without you this book would be purely fiction.

I love you.

TaBLe OF COntentS

introduction

My best friend in Spruce Grove, Alberta, was Barb Pichette, our youth pastor's wife. We bore our first children within a month of each other and quickly became friends when the kids were about nine months old. Barb and I chatted daily on the phone, detailing the escapades of our tots. Somehow my little girl got into more things, made bigger messes, and tried stunts that Barb's little boy never dreamed of. After recounting how Larisa had been prettied up for a party, then proceeded to pour a bottle of syrup over her head as she sat in the corner of the living room, Barb suggested that I start writing down Larisa's antics. I can still hear her words, "Linda, this is not normal." That night my journal began.

Years later, sitting in a women's ministry meeting in Scottsdale, Arizona, I offered up a prayer request that my father's credit cards would be located before my parents returned from vacation. This brought on several questions and laughter following the tale of my son handing out Grandpa's credit cards in Sunday School. In an encouraging response, our pastor's wife, Sharon Friend, told me, "Linda, the Lord allows you to have all these experiences so you will have something to write about." I planted that hope in my heart, knowing that someday I would write a book encouraging moms to persevere through mothering.

You are holding that book, a collection of devotions I wrote for you. My prayer is to lift you up and point you to our heavenly Father, the giver of all good gifts—including your kids. Be strengthened, reassured, and comforted that you are in the midst of the highest calling on earth—mothering. Sit back, when you have a few moments, and laugh, cry and relive with me some life lessons the Lord has taught this mother.

Find something to laugh about each day as the Lord strengthens you with His joy.

Linda Ann Crosby

mom-isms

For you did not receive a spirit that makes you a slave again to fear, but you received the spirit of sonship. And by him we cry, "Abba, Father." The Spirit himself testifies with our spirit that we are God's children. Now if we are children, then we are heirs—heirs of God and co-heirs with Christ, if indeed we share in his sufferings in order that we may also share in his glory.

Romans 8:15-17

Mom-isms are lists that I love to read because I can relate. They seem to summarize our lives in the inner sanctum. They can only be written by a woman who has been there, done that. Fancy psychologists who are childless hold nothing over us moms. Dads don't relate to these lists either. In fact, the dads I've talked to assume something is wrong with mothers who *do* relate to these lists, but they can't quite put their finger on what is wrong. We've all read them, but please grant me the opportunity to add a few of my own life experiences to the lists.

You Know You're a Mom If You . . .

- can successfully dress a hockey player, a ballerina, and a head wound—simultaneously.

- have bought socks, underwear, flip-flops, PJs and toothpaste, bearing a picture of your child's favorite character.

- drop in bed each night fully exhausted wondering, *What did I do all day?*

- need handcuffs to keep you from "helping" with the Science Fair display board.

- can feed the children, the dog, the turtles, the fish, and the crab in ten minutes flat.

- have a secret pile of coins collected from the kids' pockets on the shelf in the laundry room.

- go without a haircut for two more weeks so your child can have new shoes.

- have a purse full of Hot Wheels and size 3 emergency underwear, but no lipstick.

- hide chocolate in various kitchen cupboards . . . forget where . . . and joyously find it later!

- laugh when the water is dripping off the ceiling after bath time.

- laugh when the water is dripping through the ceiling from a rainstorm.

- read the same story 127 times because it's your child's favorite.

- can proudly wear a macaroni necklace with your best Sunday dress.

- feel like you need a black and white striped shirt to play board games with your kids.

- cry when you find an open Bible on your eight-year-old's unmade bed.

- cry when you find a layer of dust on your own Bible from under your bed.

- know you have the most rewarding job on earth.

Motherhood is not about being the best mother. It is about doing what God designed you for: nurturing, caring, loving, comforting, creating memories, building relationships and leading others to the feet of the best parent of them all, our Abba Father.

CHEESEBURGER, FRIES AND COKE, PLEASE

> *Daniel then said to the guard whom the chief official had appointed over Daniel, Hananiah, Mishael and Azariah, "Please test your servants for ten days: Give us nothing but vegetables to eat and water to drink. Then compare our appearance with that of the young men who eat the royal food, and treat your servants in accordance with what you see." So he agreed to this and tested them for ten days. At the end of the ten days they looked healthier and better nourished than any of the young men who ate the royal food.*
>
> Daniel 1:11-15

It was not my child who said, "Give us nothing but vegetables to eat and water to drink." It was Daniel, Shadrach, Meshach and Abednego who chose veggies over the king's rich food, as recorded in Daniel 1:12.

My children are much like these young men from Judah: "without any physical defect, handsome, showing aptitude for every kind of learning, well informed, quick to understand, and qualified to serve in a king's palace" (Daniel 1:4). Why then will my qualified kids not eat vegetables? What trick did the Judean mothers have over us North American mothers? "No fast-food restaurants!" is my answer.

My children could "read" the signs of fast food chains before they were potty trained. The kids' meal toys that we have accumulated could fill a laundry basket. I didn't realize that we were accustomed to convenience food until we visited Banff National Park in Alberta, Canada. We drove up to the entrance booth to inform the ranger of our plans to pass through without camping. As we pulled away, our two-year-old yelled, "Wait, Dad! He didn't take our order!" Hubby gave me a look out of the corner of his eye, which translated to *What? Where did she learn that?*

I started to think of the number of times we do drive thru. Is that the best food for my King's kids? I hate guilt, especially when it's associated with my parenting habits. Rationalization always follows guilt. I blend zucchini into the spaghetti sauce, and I add mixed vegetables to alphabet soup. They all eat broccoli. Vitamins fill in the missing nutrients, right?

For a while I thought I was achieving the diet of the Israelites with my children. Then I asked my two-year-old to leave a message for her father on our answering machine. She was supposed to say, "We'll meet you in the city at 6:00." Several rehearsals were complete. I pushed the button and Larisa yelled, "I'll have combo number three with Diet Pepsi." Realization hit me . . . along with guilt, since that is what I order at Taco Bell. Back to the U.S.D.A. nutrition pyramid for basic training.

Lord, please help me to train these kids to care for their living temples as you would.

Die To Self 101

> *In the same way, the Spirit helps us in our weakness. We do not know what we ought to pray, but the Spirit himself intercedes for us with groans that words cannot express. And he who searches our hearts knows the mind of the Spirit, because the Spirit intercedes for the saints in accordance with God's will.*
>
> Romans 8:26,27

Being married with children is like taking a crash course in Die-to-Self 101. Someone should tell expecting women that their lives will no longer be their own as soon as that bun pops out of the oven. "It's all about me" is over.

The memories that linger in my mind of the season following the difficult birth of our second child are not happy ones. It was one of the lowest times in my life. We had a little girl who was almost three. We had a newborn crier. I was 31 and often felt like I was losing my identity. I was Rick's wife, Larisa's mom and the bearer of the first grandson in the family.

Everyone in the household demanded my time, my energy, my body, my everything. I recall one late night when I had wrestled my daughter to bed and was sitting on the couch nursing the baby. Just as I started seeing the light at the end of the tunnel—a quiet evening alone—my girl yelled from the bathroom, "Mommy, please come wipe me!" Thankfully, I only needed one hand to hold the nursing babe. I had a free limb to unroll toilet paper, wipe a bum, pull up panties, flush the toilet and help with hand soap.

My family had always been teetotalers, but in my desperation, I started to question prohibition. Now I recognize that I was suffering from a mild case of postpartum depression. However, I remember planning how Rick could swing by the liquor store on the way home from work and pick up a bottle of something that would make me feel much better. I had this false assumption from TV commercials, I guess. Of course, I was also ignoring the facts that I could barely stomach cough syrup, and I gag if the toothpaste is too strong.

Desperate times call for desperate measures, so I called out to God. It was one of those irrational prayers pleading for the single days of my youth and the ability to fit into those skinny jeans I wore back then. Eventually I fell asleep, which is what I needed more than anything at that point.

God understands those prayers. He knows that mothering is taxing, demanding and intensive, but that is exactly why He called us to the task. He formed us in His image: loving, longsuffering, durable, patient and kind.

Don't give up! Rumor has it that mothers improve with age.

LET'S GO TO CHURCH

And let us consider how we may spur one another on toward love and good deeds. Let us not give up meeting together, as some are in the habit of doing, but let us encourage one another—and all the more as you see the Day approaching.

Hebrews 10:24,25

Cooped up for days. Two sick kids. Diapers overflowing the garbage can. Potato peelings drying in the sink. Clean laundry piled high waiting for hangers. The smell of maple syrup thickly hanging in the air from the half-eaten toaster waffles still on the kitchen counter.

I totally, completely and wholeheartedly relate to David's writing in Psalm 122:1 when he wrote, "I was glad when they said unto me, Let us go into the house of the LORD." The church is always clean and tidy. I've never seen toothpaste in the bathroom sink at church. The absence of toys scattered on the floor is so refreshing.

Other people will see me, so a bit of improvement is necessary. I wipe the toothpaste off my eye shadow compact and apply a thick layer of light pink to disguise darker shades. I level and even out my hairdo. I try to locate wrinkle-free clothing and trade in my comfy sweats for presentable attire.

Adult conversation. Sunday School and nursery care. I would have to be mortally wounded to face an outing to church without joy and great expectation. Socialization. Worship. I can sit alone with my husband. I can talk to the Lord without someone banging on the bathroom door. What mother wouldn't be glad to hear, "Let's go to church!"?

I've often wondered what people without children do on Sunday mornings? It must be a day to sleep in. Imagine that! And to have clothing available that is spit-up free! WOW!

We need to instill in our children the desire to attend church. Make the ride to church a joyful time of planning how each family member will bless someone at church. We have each of our kids rehearse what they could say to someone in Sunday school to brighten their day. We let the young ones slide by with "I like your shirt" or "You look nice." When the kids pass the age of single digits, they start working on personal compliments about people, not their clothing: "I'm so glad to see you this morning." "Your smile brightens the room."

Have each one report back to the family on the trip home. If we go with the idea of being a blessing instead of being blessed, we will have a greater interest and joy in our own church body. It is truly more blessed to give than to receive. We are blessed to be a blessing.

Wal-Mart Frogs

> *Give thanks to the LORD, call on his name; make known among the nations what he has done. Sing to him, sing praise to him; tell of all his wonderful acts. Glory in his holy name; let the hearts of those who seek the LORD rejoice . . . Give thanks to the LORD, for he is good; his love endures forever.*
>
> 1 Chronicles 16:8-10, 34

It was fish-tank day for the Crosby's. Our children completed the normal "I want a new pet" requirements of researching food, care, and price comparisons. Wal-Mart won the "cheapest" award, so we ventured to our neighborhood store to invest in an aquarium and all the necessary goodies that go with it.

The ten-gallon tank was chosen. Heavy discussion occurred regarding the color of pebbles. The filter landed in our basket next to the fake plants and the colorful plastic Caribbean scene for the back wall of the tank. Guppies were the fish of choice along with a bottom-feeder to keep the tank algae-free. We only needed fish flakes and we were out the door.

We were headed toward the fish food smorgasbord when my children spotted the African Dwarf Frogs. The kids went ballistic begging for the frogs. It was more than excitement; it was borderline hysteria. Their voices reached a crescendo as they whined, begged for and demanded the frogs. They were no longer listening to reason. I was getting more embarrassed as each nanosecond passed. Finally Rick had had enough and started unloading everything from the cart back to the shelf. His mouth was set in a firm straight line and I think I saw a bit of steam escape from his ears.

He marched our family to the car and somewhere along the way the kids got stealthily quiet. Dad doesn't snap very often. Doom was pending. When the fifth seatbelt clicked the lecture began. "Crosby's don't whine. Crosby's don't ask for anything twice when no is the answer. Crosby's are thankful and happy with what God has given us. Your mother and I will not be buying you anything in any store for any reason for a month."

Like the plague from Exodus 8 that incident became known as "The Frogs." Verse 14 records that, after the frogs died in Egypt, they were "piled into heaps and the land reeked of them." Wal-Mart was certainly reeking with the ungrateful hearts of my brood. To this day, if any child of mine whines or begs in a store it is halted by two words: "The Frogs." The Israelites stacked rocks as reminders of what the Lord had done. We only have to say, "The Frogs," and that is reminder enough.

We eventually did get a fish tank, and even a couple of frogs, but the kids learned a valuable lesson of being thankful for God's blessings, thanks to "The Frogs."

cleanliness is NOT always NEXT TO godliness

> *So I find this law at work: When I want to do good, evil is right there with me. For in my inner being, I delight in God's law; but I see another law at work in the members of my body, waging war against the law of my mind and making me a prisoner of the law of sin at work within my members. What a wretched man I am! Who will rescue me from this body of death? Thanks be to God—through Jesus Christ our Lord!*
>
> Romans 7:21-25a

My daughter discovered that water could be flicked off of her toothbrush onto the bathroom mirror. Of course, that was after she piled every toy she owns onto her bed. She had never put all of her toys in one place. Ever. She explained that she had filled Santa's sleigh and would deliver all the toys after lunch.

Back in the living room, I found my 11-month-old son standing on top of the coffee table. I should have been thankful. He was usually emptying the two baskets of videos and books. I made a mental note that his crib sheet needed to be changed before naptime. Obviously, whoever invented bumper pads never changed a sheet with the pads tied to the crib. If moms had three arms it might be possible.

As soon as I got the dishes out of the dishwasher and replaced them with the dirty dishes from the countertop, my daughter asked in her sweet, little voice, "Mommy, will you please color with me?" I didn't respond immediately, contemplating the new and improved messes that called my name. "Mom, I asked really nicely."

Romans 7:18b says, "I have the desire to do what is good, but I cannot carry it out." When my focus of life drifts from the children to a neat and clean house, this verse could help me justify why housework is a good work. I am reminded however that my priority is to raise warriors for God. My desire to do what is good is not carried out because it is overshadowed by my desire to do what is GREAT and RIGHT. The dirty laundry, crusty dishes and smudgy windows would still be waiting for me later. These children are precious in God's sight and deserve all the time and attention I can give them for the brief years they are entrusted to me.

"Sure, I'll color with you. Are we going to use crayons or felt pens?" *Coloring books or the walls*, I refrained from adding. Coloring is genuinely relaxing. I'll admit that I still like to color in the lines and make the edges darker than the centers. However, my style is slightly cramped when my firstborn leader keeps insisting that I use the colors she chooses.

I once saw a sign that read, "If you came to see me, come on in. If you came to see my house, please make an appointment for next week." So true!

MY LiTTLe Prince

> *The LORD is exalted over all the nations, his glory above the heavens. Who is like the LORD our God, the One who sits enthroned on high, who stoops down to look on the heavens and the earth? He raises the poor from the dust and lifts the needy from the ash heap; he seats them with princes, with the princes of their people. He settles the barren woman in her home as a happy mother of children. Praise the LORD.*
>
> Psalm 113:4-9

My 18-month-old had emptied the ashes from the fireplace onto the carpet . . . again. What possesses my children to get into every messy substance in our house? The first time this happened, it was semi-humorous—soot smeared all over his face and hands. I had to take a picture for my scrapbook. The second time, I threw him into the tub without looking for the camera. I was visibly upset: tight lips, glaring eyes, short breaths. It was not even slightly funny. Then he smiled a huge toothy grin and yelled, "Cheese!"

I cleaned the child, his clothes, the carpet and my clothes. Then I plopped down at the kitchen table exhausted. My Bible was open to Psalms. Something caught my eye: "He . . . lifts the needy from the ash heap; he seats them with princes . . . He settles the barren woman in her home as a *happy* mother of children" (Psalm 113:7-9b, emphasis added).

God must have had a twinkle of laughter in his eye when He prompted David to write that verse for me. For that day. For strength. For a laugh. I'm sure King David was looking down from heaven finally realizing why he wrote those words so many years ago.

Keep your Bible handy. Better yet, keep many Bibles handy in various places around your house. The bathroom is a great place, as well as next to the couch. And don't forget the car. We can never get enough of God's Word or His timely encouragement during our busy days.

A box of Bible quiz cards sits on our kitchen table as another means of getting God's truth into our hearts. Frequently I test the children's knowledge and we learn together. Several days ago I read card 275: What is sin? Good question. I formulated the answer in my head, then flipped the card over to see how my Christian education had paid off. Not too well that time. The answer: Sin is refusing to do God's will as revealed by His Word and His Spirit.

The word *refusing* jumped off the card and smacked me between the eyes. Sin is a choice. The psalmist instructs us in Psalm 119:11 to hide God's Word in our hearts so we won't sin against Him. When I neglect Scripture reading I'm refusing to obey what has been revealed to me.

Lord, give me strength to stop refusing. Help me live by what You have revealed to me in Your Word.

GOD'S COMMANDS

> *And God spoke all these words: . . . You shall have no other gods before me. You shall not make for yourself an idol . . . You shall not misuse the name of the LORD your God . . . Remember the Sabbath day by keeping it holy . . . Honor your father and your mother . . . You shall not murder. You shall not commit adultery. You shall not steal. You shall not give false testimony against your neighbor. You shall not covet.*
>
> Exodus 20:1-17

When my children were younger, I decided to start teaching them the Ten Commandments from Exodus 20. Carefully adjusting the laws of God to a preschool level, I came up with a shortened version that I thought the kids would understand.

1. There is only one God.

2. Don't worship anything else.

3. Don't say bad words.

4. Go to church on Sunday.

5. Obey your parents.

6. Don't kill.

7. Only do hugging and kissing with the one you married.

8. Don't steal.

9. Don't lie.

10. Be happy with what you have.

I made a little chart and drew pictures to help the kids remember these commands. The children were very interested and could tell me about each one. We had lengthy discussions—for preschoolers anyway—about different situations where people disobeyed God's commands and what happened to them. My daughter asked why some people don't keep the first person they married. These were hard questions to answer. I tried to explain that bad things sometimes happen to God's children. Sometimes we make bad decisions. Situations come up that are bad, but God helps us to make the best decision in a bad circumstance.

We were driving with the windows down one sunny day, and we pulled up to a stop light next to a man in a convertible who was smoking. My daughter was in the backseat by the window right next to the smoker. After analyzing him for a long time she yelled, "You aren't a bad person. It's just a bad habit." Saved by a green light! Avoiding eye contact with the man, I let him speed away as my car crept over the crosswalk.

It is inspiring when your kids recognize bad habits in the life of others. It is humbling when God uses your children to point out discrepancies between what you are teaching them and what you are living.

The Ten Commandments chart was posted next to the kitchen table so we could see it every day. During lunch one day, my daughter was carefully studying each one. After a while, she looked at me and asked, "Mom, when Dad takes the newspaper from McDonalds, is he breaking God's command about stealing?" Instead of answering, I dialed my husband's work number and handed the phone to her. It was an entertaining conversation for me to listen in on. Live what you believe!

THE WRITING ON THE WALL

As they [King Belshazzar and a thousand of his nobles] drank the wine, they praised the gods of gold and silver, of bronze, iron, wood and stone. Suddenly the fingers of a human hand appeared and wrote on the plaster of the wall, near the lampstand in the royal palace. The king watched the hand as it wrote. His face turned pale and he was so frightened that his knees knocked together and his legs gave way. The king called out . . . "Whoever reads this writing and tells me what it means will be clothed in purple and have a gold chain placed around his neck, and he will be made the third highest ruler in the kingdom." . . . Then Daniel answered the king, "You may keep your gifts for yourself and give your rewards to someone else. Nevertheless, I will read the writing for the king and tell him what it means."

Daniel 5:4-7a, 17

It was King Belshazzar who saw "the fingers of a human hand" appear and write on the plaster of the wall in the royal palace.

It was my child who took crayons in her hand and wrote on the wall in her bedroom (not to mention the closet doors, a table and a couple of dolls).

It was King Belshazzar who was so frightened that his face turned pale, his knees knocked together and his legs gave way (vs. 6).

It was my child, upon hearing me approach, who became pale; her knees knocked, and her pulse quickened.

It was King Belshazzar who was found wanting by God and was slain that very night (vs. 27, 30).

It was my child who was found guilty and, by the grace of God, was not slain that very night. Instead she learned all about soft-scrub cleanser, a scrub brush, and elbow grease.

That was the one and only time there was writing on the wall in my home . . . or so I thought. Before going to bed a week or so later, I went searching for my toothbrush. I found it in my child's room on the floor next to her sweet, angelic sleeping form. The bristles were hardened due to a foreign substance that had been applied in my absence. The next day I asked what she had put in it. "Soap," she replied. "I had to scrub something off the wall." Well, at least she was cleaning up after herself. Note to self: Buy a new toothbrush.

We need to overlook our children's shortcomings and focus on their correct behaviors. Build up those kids when they aim to please, and even when they don't. There are times when I have to make a concentrated effort to find the good that is placed there by God in each of them. It's easy to find the bad. But we need to focus on the good. We may have to search thoroughly to praise each one, especially on the rough days. Positive parenting is all about determining our focus.

I've heard it said that a youngster who does nothing as a child will do nothing as an adult. If that is true, I can't wait to see the myriad of creative things my kids will be doing as adults.

It may not always be in the way we expect, but progress is being made in this journey through motherhood. If a picture paints a thousand words, then there's a novel on the family room wall. Hallelujah!

Blackie Honey Bunny

Our family had very few pets while we were growing up: one hamster, a kitty, a rabbit and a few fish. My husband's experience was much the same, although it was three dogs throughout his childhood: Winkey, Winkie #2 and Winkee #3. We never thought much about getting pets for our children . . . until the begging began.

It all started with Blackie Honey Bunny Crosby. My kindergarten-aged daughter, Larisa, wanted a bunny worse than life itself. A prime learning experience in the palm of my hand, I said O.K. with several strings attached. 1. Mommy was not going to feed the bunny. 2. Mommy was not going to clean up after the bunny. 3. Most importantly, Mommy was not going to be blamed when the bunny was neglected. With Bible in hand and child at my knee, I read from Proverbs 12:10: "A righteous man cares for the needs of his animal." Thus began the Crosby Pet Purchasing Requirements.

Not being a huge animal lover myself, I set some lofty goals for my daughter to reach before Bugs came to live with us, secretly hoping her interest would wane. With soft fur in her reach, Larisa plodded through building a bunny cage and painting a faded playhouse red with white trim so the bunny would have a barn. Next, she researched pet care and gave her father and me an oral report on rabbits and their needs. She listed all of the foods rabbits eat and asked our grocery store's produce manager if she could have discarded veggies each week. She listed all of the supplies necessary and made a cost-comparison sheet with prices from two stores. She phoned a vet to find prices for emergency care and volunteered at a rabbit shelter. Finally she set up a schedule for feeding and cleaning, then came to me with my "lofty" goals successfully checked off.

God knew exactly when she would complete her tasks. He had a sign posted along our route to the library which stated: Free Rabbits. To our benefit, it turned out to be a 4-H project gone wild!

After three long months of working, our daughter was the proud master of an ebony Rex with silver eyes and one floppy ear—not a pure breed to be sure. Pride of ownership beamed forth for two years as she diligently cared for Blackie's needs and proved herself a righteous person.

The abilities of a six-year-old with a dream are unfathomable. Never underestimate the power of a dream.

Keep Looking Up

> *I lift up my eyes to the hills—where does my help come from? My help comes from the LORD, the Maker of heaven and earth. He will not let your foot slip—he who watches over you will not slumber; indeed, he who watches over Israel will neither slumber nor sleep. The LORD watches over you—the LORD is your shade at your right hand; the sun will not harm you by day, nor the moon by night. The LORD will keep you from all harm—he will watch over your life; the LORD will watch over your coming and going both now and forevermore.*
>
> Psalm 121:1-8

While sitting on the couch surrounded by my blessed tots, I counted 48 items strewn on the floor. Scattered there without a care were three socks, Thomas the Tank Engine, Hot Wheels, kitchen utensils (actually microphones from air-band performances), Barbie shoes, Sunday school crafts, the plastic shield of faith from the Armor of God play set, scattered Cheerios and three children. Sometimes I think the sole job description for my children should be "Movers of Miscellaneous Items." That's really all they do. Pick it up. Walk to a different location. Put it down. Pick up something else. Walk to a different location. Put it down. And so on. And so on.

I'm convinced that this scenario occurred in King David's palace: Absalom, toddling through the throne room, picks up the scepter. He drags it out to the courtyard and sets it down by the fountain. He sees rocks by the well, picks them up and heads back for the throne room. He lays the rocks by the steps in front of the throne. And so on. And so on. This may be what prompted King David to write Psalm 121:1-2: "I lift up my eyes to the hills—where does my help come from? My help comes from the LORD, the Maker of heaven and earth."

It is frustrating to move from one clean-up job to the next with no end in sight. I prefer to call this three-on-one. I tidy the living room; my three kids are emptying the dresser in the bedroom. I go to straighten the dresser drawers; they move to the bathroom. It's never ending: three messing, one cleaning.

If we keep our eyes on the messes we will never look into the precious faces of the "masters of disaster" that God gave us. Clear a space on the carpet. Lie on the floor and look straight up. It will make you feel better because you can't see the scattering of loose articles. Before you know it, those little "arrows that fill your quiver" will be staring in your face. They will probably be wondering if they should call 9-1-1. This will momentarily get your focus on the most valuable gems in your life—your children.

Mothering is the most important job on earth. When we get sidetracked, we must remember our help comes from the Lord.

My Mom Breaks the Law!

> *Likewise, teach the older women to be reverent in the way they live, not to be slanderers or addicted to much wine, but to teach what is good. Then they can train the younger women to love their husbands and children, to be self-controlled and pure, to be busy at home, to be kind, and to be subject to their husbands, so that no one will malign the word of God.*
>
> Titus 2:3-5

When Larisa was six, she enjoyed being able to read street signs. It thrilled her so much that she read out loud every sign we passed. I found it humorous to listen to her pronounce words that I hadn't sounded out in thirty-something years. My favorite: For Union Hills Drive she said, "Onion Hills Drive."

We were stopped at a light next to a bright red billboard. She slowly read, "Don't . . . drink . . . and . . . drive." She was trying to wrap her brain around the reasoning behind the message, and finally asked, "Why?" I told her drinking and driving was against the law.

Aghast, she spit out, "Mom! You drink and drive all the time!" She was so right. I drink water, soda, smoothies, milk, slushies, and even juice while I drive.

How do you explain being drunk to a child? It went something like this: "When grape juice goes bad, it turns into alcohol. Alcohol doesn't taste very good, and it makes your thinking fuzzy. When people drink too much alcohol, they don't have control of what they say or do. It makes their driving very dangerous. They could get in an accident and die or even kill someone else." Feeling the need to excuse my actions, I ended with, "It's O.K. to drink pop or water while you're driving."

Assuming a discussion is over with a six-year-old is like shoveling the walk while it's still snowing. My thought pattern went off in another direction, going over pertinent information for my day, when she asked, "So, if alcohol tastes bad and makes your brain not work . . . why do people drink it?" I explained that some people drink alcohol so they can forget all the problems in their lives. They turn to alcohol instead of to God.

Titus 2:3 says, "Teach the older women to be reverent in the way they live, not to be slanderers or addicted to much wine, but to teach what is good." While feeling a bit self-righteous that our family is dry, it dawned on me that being a slanderer was mentioned before being addicted to much wine. The dictionary defines slander as "a false report maliciously uttered and tending to injure the reputation of a person."

Slandering doesn't taste good on our lips, and it makes our thinking fuzzy about others. Instead of turning to slander, we need to turn to God and pray for those around us.

THE WEEK OF TRIALS

> *[Jesus took the apostles] with him and they withdrew by themselves to a town called Bethsaida, but the crowds learned about it and followed him. He welcomed them and spoke to them about the kingdom of God, and healed those who needed healing.*
>
> Luke 9:10b-11

In the two years that Rick had a pager, no emergency arose for me to call it until The Week of Trials, as it came to be known. First, my three-year-old son Austin got stung by a scorpion. I dialed 9-1-1 on Rick's pager. To my utter shock, he didn't call back for four hours. Later he told me that in some locations his pager didn't work. Just great!

Two days later Keeve, our one-year-old, suffered a gouge on his forehead. Head wounds bleed like opened fire hydrants. After an hour of trying to stop the bleeding I dialed 9-1-1 on Rick's pager to see if he thought I should take Keeve to the emergency room. To my dismay, Rick didn't call me, but came home after another hour and a half. Once again, I explained that 9-1-1 means EMERGENCY and that he should call back right away.

Two days after that, six-year-old Larisa decided to ride a skateboard down the slide in our backyard. She slammed the ground so hard she went into shock. She screamed, turned blue and passed out. I called the real 9-1-1 that time and paramedics arrived to check her back for spinal injuries. I called Rick's pager and dialed 9-1-1 for the third time in five days.

While two firemen probed Larisa's back, another one came to me and mentioned that he could hear crying in the backyard. I glanced out the back door to see Keeve doing battle with a rosebush. He was losing. The thorns had grabbed his shirt and he had tried to escape by twisting his body, causing scratches and a bit of blood. As I was carefully peeling him out of the rosebush the phone rang. My "hello" was met with Rick's stern voice, "Why in the world are you dialing 9-1-1 on my pager *again*?" At least he called right away!

I'm usually pretty steady on the female emotional roller coaster, but his question did me in. I yelled in the phone, "MAYBE BECAUSE THE PARAMEDICS ARE HERE!" "Oh." That was it? Just, "Oh." Then it dawned on me: What could Rick do anyway? I should have been calling Jesus, the one who "healed those who needed healing" (Luke 9:11c). The reference is by no means a coincidence. He is the answer to any emergency that arises: physical, emotional, mental, spiritual. We simply need to turn to Him. He's just a (phone) call away.

No Driving Experience Necessary

> *Blessed is the man who does not walk in the counsel of the wicked or stand in the way of sinners or sit in the seat of mockers. But his delight is in the law of the LORD, and on his law he meditates day and night. He is like a tree planted by streams of water, which yields its fruit in season and whose leaf does not wither. Whatever he does prospers . . . For the LORD watches over the way of the righteous, but the way of the wicked will perish.*
>
> Psalm 1:1-3, 6

Escaping the heat is a major summer pastime in Phoenix. With the mercury soaring well into the one-hundred-teens, we jumped at the opportunity to go boating with some friends. Our kids needed life jackets, so I called my friend Kimberly who said we could borrow their three. When I arrived at her house to pick them up, I hopped out and left the van running so the kids would stay cool in the air-conditioned vehicle.

At the door I chatted for two or three minutes then turned to walk back to the van with the life jackets in tow . . . but the van wasn't where I had left it. My daughter Larisa, the firstborn, our very own crime-scene investigator, was running across the lawn frantically yelling and waving her arms above her head. Most of what she said was unintelligible to me, but I quickly ascertained that her four-year-old brother, Austin, had experienced the thrill of driving for the first time. My heart lurched and lodged in my throat as I wondered if I still had three living children.

Austin had unbuckled himself from his car seat and leaped into the driver's seat the second I left the vehicle. On his knees at the helm he shifted into reverse and gradually rolled down the driveway across the road and up a curb. The only thing that stopped him from crashing into the house was a bright yellow fire hydrant, which was left standing at a 35-degree angle. Thankfully, it wasn't impersonating Old Faithful.

If that wasn't enough excitement for him, Austin then shifted into drive, bounced down off the curb and headed straight for the house caddie-corner from the hydrant. He narrowly bypassed a parked car on his way toward the next door neighbor's house, when he somehow slammed the gear shift into "P" (for Praise God!). Imagine the adrenaline rush he was enjoying! He absolutely could not stop giggling out of nervousness.

That was the day I figured out that our family was counted in heaven as "righteous." Psalm 1:6a tells us that "the LORD watches over the way of the righteous." God had a fleet of angels assigned to us that day. And they had their work cut out for them.

Several lessons we learned:

1. Never leave children in a running vehicle (unless you don't mind being on the 6:00 news).

2. Count your blessings, for the Lord is watching over you.

3. Driver's training is a worthwhile investment.

If folly was bound up in the heart of my child, I think he untied it.

grocery store granDma

> *But now a righteousness from God, apart from law, has been made known, to which the Law and the Prophets testify. This righteousness from God comes through faith in Jesus Christ to all who believe. There is no difference, for all have sinned and fall short of the glory of God, and are justified freely by his grace through the redemption that came by Christ Jesus.*
>
> Romans 3:21-24

My three little personal shoppers were busily making purchasing recommendations in the pasta aisle of the grocery store one day, when an elderly woman with stooped shoulders and cotton-white hair shuffled toward us. She was glowing with delight, admiring my three angels. My pride puffed up a bit, as my kids were clean and shiny with their hair combed to perfection. This is rarely the case, so the woman's rosy-cheeked smile was a blessing to me.

"You have a beautiful family," she graciously offered. Before I could thank her, my middle son who is normally quite timid blurted out, "I'm Austin." Pointing to his brother he added, "And this is Keeve." This warmed the woman's heart and she took a minute to converse with my brood. She told the boys they had nice names and then spoke kindly to my daughter. She turned to me again and smiled before she started on her way. There was ten feet between us when my son yelled, "My daddy drives a fancy Cadillac!" At this, the woman threw her head back and laughed wholeheartedly, as did I.

Through the rest of the produce section and the dairy aisle I pondered the many reasons why children give out such fascinating facts to strangers. Was I like this as a kid, telling people in the grocery store that my dad wore a flashlight on his head to fix the TV, or that my mom owned her own bowling ball?

My thoughts were similar to Christ's in Luke 7:31-32. Jesus was talking about people who were complaining. "To what, then, can I compare the people of this generation? What are they like? They are like children sitting in the marketplace and calling out . . . " These men that Jesus spoke of could not be serious in the concerns of their own souls. He compared them to children who are full of play and find it difficult to be serious and/or quiet. Kids like mine that give out useless information in the market.

God filled our kids with spontaneity to keep us on our toes. We need to remember that kids are kids, and there is hardly any logic behind their actions and reactions. When it comes to the life-or-death decision of salvation, however, we need to instruct our children in all seriousness about their sin, God's forgiveness, and their need to call upon His name to be saved.

THE Beginning OF Crosby's Petting Zoo

> *But the fruit of the Spirit is love, joy, peace, patience, kindness, goodness, faithfulness, gentleness and self-control. Against such things there is no law. Those who belong to Christ Jesus have crucified the sinful nature with its passions and desires. Since we live by the Spirit, let us keep in step with the Spirit. Let us not become conceited, provoking and envying each other.*
>
> Galatians 5:22-26

Most kids want a pet or two, but my children were born with a zookeeper mentality. I never should have read Genesis 1:26 to my brood. God said, "Let us make man in our image, in our likeness, and let them rule over the fish of the sea and the birds of the air, over the livestock, over all the earth, and over all the creatures that move along the ground." This verse became an inventory list in their heads, a new mission to be accomplished.

It all started with three Wal-Mart guppies, the "fish in the sea". Yet another lesson from God's creation unfolded in our ten-gallon tank . . . live birth! Daily three pairs of curious eyes noted the enlarging belly of mama guppy. With a translucent tummy, the dark eyes of the fry were visible and intriguing. The glorious day arrived and I was roused from peaceful dreams to shouts of, "Mama guppy is having her babies!" "Push! Push!" I heard my daughter yell. Pandemonium of three voices followed with, "There it is!" "Look how small it is!" and "I can't see it!" Guppies immediately need to swim to the surface for an initial breath of air, to which my children yelled, "Swim! Swim!" So the morning went on, "Push! . . . Swim!"

At one point my daughter turned to me and remarked, "I can't believe I'm letting a guppy control my emotions!" This would have been an unusual statement to most parents, but we had been repeatedly telling Larisa that she didn't need to let others control her emotions. *She* needed to control them. Flying off the handle at her brothers was unacceptable and self-control was the fruit of the Spirit that she needed. I silently thanked the Lord for using a guppy to help her understand.

Mama guppy produced 31 "arrows from her quiver" that morning. Quite an accomplishment, if you ask me. Albeit, watching live guppy birth is fascinating, we were quickly realizing that the fish were making rules of their own without consulting us first. From three guppies to 34 to 56 was not my idea of control. We were not ruling the fish of the sea. Yet another job title was added to my resume: Guppy Relocation Specialist. Guppies are like zucchini. You end up with so many that you run out of friends to give them to.

FUNERAL SONGS

> *Archers shot King Josiah, and he told his officers, "Take me away; I am badly wounded." So they took him out of his chariot, put him in the other chariot he had and brought him to Jerusalem, where he died. He was buried in the tombs of his fathers, and all Judah and Jerusalem mourned for him. Jeremiah composed laments for Josiah, and to this day all the men and women singers commemorate Josiah in the laments. These became a tradition in Israel and are written in the Laments.*
>
> 2 Chronicles 35:23-25

As I read 2 Chronicles 35:25 about the prophet Jeremiah composing sorrowful funeral songs for Josiah, I was reminded of a family burial with songs of a different sort.

Our story begins with the death of our beloved rabbit Blackie Honey Bunny. He hadn't been put in his cage for the night and some kind of animal came into the yard and killed him. I was thankful the Lord had me, not the children, discover the dead rabbit on the back lawn.

I rang my husband's cell phone not knowing that he was in a flight briefing meeting at the airport. After a rundown from the home front, I asked him what I should do about the bunny. Trying not to disturb the other pilots, he cupped his hand over the phone and whispered, "Dig a hole and put the body in it." "O.K. Bye."

I found the shovel and started digging, but eight inches down into the ground the shovel hit solid slate. I called Rick again. "I hit rock. It's not deep enough," I whispered. "Put the body in a bag. I'll deal with it later." Click.

Blackie was double bagged in black lawn and garden bags and placed by the trash. With that done, I hurried into the house to pack for a week-long vacation at the cabin. For the remainder of the day my mind was a flurry of groceries, flannel jammies, and sleeping bags.

We left for the trip as soon as Rick arrived home. It wasn't until we were an hour down the road that my eyes flew open and I whispered to my husband, "OH NO! The rabbit!" He casually replied, "I took care of it." Relief washed over me. "Good. What did you do with it?" To my complete shock, he flicked his head back and said, "It's in the back. We'll bury it at the cabin." I slowly shook my head and mumbled, "Normal people don't take dead pets on vacation."

Children need closure after the death of a pet. Likewise they need to be taught respect for God's creatures, so we had a burial and sang "Little Bunny Foo Foo," "Here Comes Peter Cottontail" and "The Bunny Song" from Veggie Tales. My daughter prayed a prayer of thanksgiving to the Lord for the time she had with Blackie then threw a bouquet of wildflowers on top of her rabbit. That was her first experience with death— a sad but real part of life.

A Bird in the Hand is Too Many

> *May the LORD answer you when you are in distress; may the name of the God of Jacob protect you. May he send you help from the sanctuary and grant you support from Zion. May he remember all your sacrifices and accept your burnt offerings. May he give you the desire of your heart and make all your plans succeed. We will shout for joy when you are victorious and will lift up our banners in the name of our God.*
>
> Psalm 20:1-5

After our fish lesson came, "Let them rule . . . the birds in the air (Genesis 1:26b)." Pets are not my cup of tea, but birds are *definitely* not my idea of a good time. Larisa was eight years old when a pet bird became necessary for her happiness. Adamantly I said, "No way!" But this did not hamper my daughter's desire to catch a bird.

Our backyard was a bird sanctuary with 13 trees, most frequently visited by mourning doves, house wrens and thrashers. Methodically Larisa built a trap out of a green plastic milk crate, taping the handle holes closed with packing tape. She located a stick shaped like a "Y" to hold one side off the ground. Next she tied variegated rainbow colored yarn to the stick and propped up the crate. Carefully a pile of bird seed was placed under the trap and the yarn led through the backdoor. This was the perfect setup, as our backdoor was all glass and birds couldn't see into the house.

Honestly, I didn't think she would be able to catch a bird. I should have remembered that a child's persistence and determination had proven me wrong before. After 45 minutes of sitting cross-legged on the cold tile floor, she yanked the string and successfully caught a mourning dove in her milk crate trap. She was ruling the birds of the air.

Being a responsible pet owner, she added more food and a little cup of water for the dove trapped in the crate. She begged. She pleaded. It didn't work. Not that time. I explained that it was a wild bird that God made to fly. It couldn't do what God made it to do if she kept it under her crate. At dusk she let it go and returned to the house with slumped shoulders.

Just as the dove had a purpose for life, so do each of our children. The key to an individual's purpose is wrapped up in what that person truly loves to do. Psalm 20:4 says, "May [God] give you the desire of your heart and make all your plans succeed." I believe I'm raising either a veterinarian, a lion tamer or another Dr. Doolittle. What do your children love to do? Encourage them in their heart's desire and lead them to their whole purpose.

iF a man will not work

> *For even when we were with you, we gave you this rule:
> "If a man will not work, he shall not eat." We hear that
> some among you are idle. They are not busy; they are
> busybodies. Such people we command and urge in the
> Lord Jesus Christ to settle down and earn the bread
> they eat. And as for you, brothers, never tire of doing
> what is right.*
>
> 2 Thessalonians 3:10-13

You can call snails "escargot," but they're still snails. It's
the same with chores. Call them family blessings or daily helps.
It doesn't matter. They are still chores and are called "chores"
in this house.

My husband and I are in agreement that our children must
have a working knowledge of running a household. This in mind,
I made a list of every chore and noted the number of times per
week each should be done. I divided the tasks between myself
and the children and the rest is history. Oh, don't go thinking it
went over smoothly! Far from it.

Knowing my children's ability to question anything new in
their lives, I prepared a chore chart with a Bible verse in bold
letters across the top. "If a man will not work, he shall not eat"
(2 Thessalonians 3:10b). Sounds harsh, but it's scriptural.

Yes, they tested God's Word, the chore chart, and my God-given authority. The initial perpetrators: my male offspring. At 10:30 a.m. I announced it was room cleaning time, gave a few pointers, and left the room with a smug look on my face. Thirty minutes later, I noticed new toys were introduced to the mix. Gently I reminded them to clean, not play.

At noon the boys showed up in the kitchen wondering what was for lunch. "Egg salad sandwiches, grapes, chips, applesauce, and chocolate milk," I delivered with the efficiency of a Denny's waitress. They looked pleased and headed for the table. Broadcasting loudly from the chore chart on the fridge, I read the verse: "IF A MAN WILL NOT WORK, HE SHALL NOT EAT." I've been known to do something weird once in a while, so the boys thought nothing of it.

As I was putting their plates in Ziploc bags they asked what I was up to. Rhetorical questions are another one of my gifts. "Did you work cleaning your room? No. Do you get to eat without working? No. Is your room still a mess? Yes. Are you hungry? Yes. Then go clean your room." I just love it when their eyes get wide.

Hunger got the best of them around 2:30 in the afternoon and the room was instantly spotless. The sandwiches were a bit soggy, the chips had drifted into the applesauce, but my hardworking little men ate without a complaint and seldom tested 2 Thessalonians 3:10 again.

Happy Gas, Please!

> *Ask and it will be given to you; seek and you will find; knock and the door will be opened to you. For everyone who asks receives; he who seeks finds; and to him who knocks, the door will be opened. Which of you, if his son asks for bread, will give him a stone? Or if he asks for a fish, will give him a snake? If you, then, though you are evil, know how to give good gifts to your children, how much more will your Father in heaven give good gifts to those who ask him!*
>
> Matthew 7:7-11

Moms are used to cold meals, lukewarm showers and potato chip crumbs. We get what is leftover. This is because a mother's heart always wants to make sure the needs of her children are met before her own. We don't do it to be martyrs. We do it because we love our families. We want the best for our kids. We want to provide them with more than we had.

Sitting in the dentist chair after many months of absence, I told my dentist that we had been focusing on taking care of the children's teeth. We had completed several visits with fillings, sealant and orthodontic consultations, and the kids were all taken care of for the time being. It was my turn. My ship had finally come in. It was as good as when the Home Depot paint technician finally calls my number to mix my paint. I felt like yelling, "Bingo!"

The "it's all about me" syndrome rapidly faded as my dentist examined my X-rays and was formulating a strategic plan of attack. I knew it couldn't be positive news with the necessity of a plan of attack. She gingerly explained to me that the enamel next to my gums on all of my lower molars was wearing away. How could that be? I brush my teeth and floss like the Energizer Bunny. If that didn't make my day, she questioned, "Did you have your children close together? Sometimes that causes a chemical reaction that destroys the enamel." WHAT? There was another side effect of having children that no one told me about? This wasn't listed in *What to Expect When You're Expecting*.

Over the following months I spent many hours in the dentist's chair. I told her that, despite the Novocain shots, this was my personal time without my children. It was supposed to be relaxing. My only request: "Use lots of happy gas, please."

I know. I know. There is always a silver lining. In this case though, along with the enamel, it was the silver fillings that needed to be replaced with crowns. This gave new meaning to Matthew 7:11 where our Father in heaven gives good gifts to those who ask him. We asked for children. The Lord gave us three kids and threw in my new teeth! Is there no end to the added benefits of having children?

WANTED: OUTLAW CARRYING A KNIFE

> *When they reached the place God had told him about, Abraham built an altar there and arranged the wood on it. He bound his son Isaac and laid him on the altar, on top of the wood. Then he reached out his hand and took the knife to slay his son. But the angel of the LORD called out to him from heaven, "Abraham! Abraham!" "Here I am," he replied. "Do not lay a hand on the boy," he said. "Do not do anything to him. Now I know that you fear God, because you have not withheld from me your son, your only son."*
>
> Genesis 22:9-12

It was a pearl-sided, spring-loaded pocket knife with a four-inch blade. Austin cherished his treasured gift as any six-year-old boy would, who was found responsible enough to own one. His chest enlarged as he showed others how it opened and closed. He sharpened it repeatedly, ready for anything: chopping down a sapling, battling an intruder, or killing a wild animal. He carried it everywhere. With his knife he could conquer all.

Much training and warning transpired before Austin's unsupervised knife days. He was educated on handling, opening and closing, cleaning and throwing. My husband thought he had covered all the dos and don'ts. He somehow overlooked a couple: #27—Don't cut the screens off the neighbor's house. (That's another story!) #28—Don't cut up all the fruit on our citrus trees unless you're having a lemonade stand.

Rain was sprinkling when Austin went out to play with his friend Duncan under the grapefruit tree in our side yard. The tree was huge and the foliage so dense the rain couldn't penetrate. It was their fort, free from the elements, as they dreamed of crossing the South Seas in search of treasure.

The following day I ventured into the yard to retrieve the mail. As I turned back toward the house, I froze as I took in 30 to 40 chopped-up grapefruits all over the neighbor's roof. I stormed into the house looking for the outlaw. It wasn't so much anger within me; it was duty and responsibility. I grabbed the knife from Austin and fear filled his eyes. I felt like Abraham. He had a knife in his hand ready to slay his son when the Lord called out from heaven saying, "Do not lay a hand on the boy" (Genesis 22:12). No hand was laid on Isaac . . . or Austin.

With trash bag in hand, Austin went out to pick up the mangled fruit that was on the ground in our yard and the neighbor's. Next I went with him to knock on their door and inform them of Austin's clean-up duty. He apologized and went to work. I scraped the grapefruit off the roof with a hockey stick and he bagged 'em.

We filled two trash bags that day—the last two trash bags we will ever fill with chopped-up grapefruit. These days, Austin is weighing the consequences before choosing knife wielding activities, but mostly he is using his pearl-sided, spring-loaded pocket knife for whittling.

When life hands you lemons, leave them on the tree until you need them.

grandma grunfeld

> *I have learned to be content whatever the circumstances.
> I know what it is to be in need, and I know what it is to
> have plenty. I have learned the secret of being content
> in any and every situation, whether well fed or hungry,
> whether living in plenty or in want. I can do everything
> through him who gives me strength.*
>
> Philippians 4:11-13

Across the street from us lived a wonderful, little Jewish woman whom we lovingly called Grandma Grunfeld. She lived alone and loved visiting with our children and hearing all they had to say. She was so thoughtful, always remembering the kids' birthdays and keeping a stash of candy just for them in her linen closet.

Grandma Grunfeld gave me much food-for-thought through the years. We had a fair-sized yard with many well established trees and shrubs that required constant attention. After a tiring day of pruning shrubs and our overly prolific olive trees, I was sitting on a planter taking a break when Grandma Grunfeld shuffled out to collect her mail. She commented on all the clippings on the ground and I made some unthankful remark about our unending yard work. She stopped in her tracks and replied just as sweetly as she made every comment, "Just be thankful you can still do the work!" So true!

Clipping coupons was Grandma Grunfeld's special blessing for all of her neighbors and friends at her synagogue. She carefully selected diapers, Spaghettios, and Go-gurt coupons for us while we were neighbors. She also ordered magazine subscriptions "for herself," but would give them to the kids shortly after they made an appearance in her mailbox.

One year when May Day arrived I explained to my daughter the tradition of leaving flowers at someone's doorstep. Larisa thoughtfully suggested that we leave flowers for Grandma Grunfeld, so we readied six cans in a basket and collected flowers. With a bow attached to the handle, we strolled across Yucca Street to be met with joy and Grandma Grunfeld's favorite expression, "Terrific!" She asked if all the beautiful flowers were from our yard. Nine-year-old Larisa truthfully responded, "All of them are except for those dark pink ones. We stole those from over our back fence." True, they did originate from our back neighbor's yard. But is it stealing if they hang five feet into our yard?

Grandma Grunfeld has not had an easy life, being a Holocaust survivor, a widow, and now having health challenges. She is, however, much like the apostle Paul who wrote in Philippians 4:11 that he had "learned to be content whatever the circumstances." God used one of his chosen people to teach us many valuable life lessons while we were neighbors. Who has God placed in the house across the street from you to help you learn some of life's most valuable lessons?

Pioneer, Arizona

> *And God said, "Let the water under the sky be gathered to one place, and let dry ground appear." And it was so. God called the dry ground "land," and the gathered waters he called "seas." And God saw that is was good. Then God said, "Let the land produce vegetation: seed-bearing plants and trees on the land that bear fruit with seed in it, according to their various kinds." And it was so. The land produced vegetation: plants bearing seed according to their kinds and trees bearing fruit with seed in it according to their kinds. And God saw that is was good. And there was evening, and there was morning—the third day.*
>
> Genesis 1:9-13

My kids and I spent a day at Pioneer, Arizona—a dusty, old frontier town just north of Phoenix. We all dressed up (even me, to my children's amusement!), sat in the school house for a looooonnnng lesson, jumped rope, rolled hoops with sticks, played tug-of-war, watched a shoot-out, sat on blankets and ate out of our baskets on the village green, danced the Virginia Reel, churned butter, dipped candles, made rope and watched the blacksmith make nails. It was AWESOME!

However, the day didn't go exactly as I had planned. I had arranged to have our 4-year-old son, Keeve, stay with Grandma. Unfortunately, Grandma got the 24-hour-very-inconvenient-for-me flu bug. So I scraped together another set of suspenders, knee socks and knickers and kept reminding myself that in the pioneer days Grandma wasn't always available to keep the kiddies.

My husband later asked how Keeve managed. I told him that he did what every 4-year-old pioneer kid would do—he ate rocks, picked up every stick he could find, jumped in the mud, laughed hard, pulled up grass, banged on windows, snapped his brother's suspenders, pulled a board off an old fence, asked what *every* tombstone in the cemetery said, chased bugs, rolled in the dirt, talked loudly when everyone else was quiet, sat on the 100-year-old couches that had ropes across them (so we wouldn't sit on them), crowed with the rooster, scared a few chickens and generally enjoyed himself.

Keeve was never bored. It made me think about his technologically advanced life . . . that isn't nearly as much fun as being outside in God's creation. Kids need fresh air and sunshine. They also need rain, snow, mud, and lightning to have a well-rounded upbringing. Kids need to experience sleeping under the stars, freezing in a sleeping bag all night, and having their ankles nibbled by wild trout.

We take the opportunity to escape to God's wilderness every chance we get. There is nothing that Disneyland can produce that is as awesome as what God has made in Carlsbad Caverns or the Grand Canyon. Take a peak in the nearest national park. Go fishing. Find some sand dunes to roll down. Get out and live life with your kids in God's world. Genesis 1:9-13 tells us about the third day of creation when God made the earth for us. The end of verse 12 reads, "And God saw that it was good." Can I hear an "Amen"?

when i was your age

*Hear, O Israel: The LORD our God, the LORD is one. Love
the LORD your God with all your heart and with all your
soul and with all your strength. These commandments
that I give you today are to be upon your hearts. Impress
them on your children. Talk about them when you sit at
home and when you walk along the road, when you lie
down and when you get up. Tie them as symbols on your
hands and bind them on your foreheads. Write them on
the doorframes of your houses and on your gates.*

Deuteronomy 6:4-9

One house we lived in had a playhouse in a gigantic
mulberry tree in the backyard. Not only did it sleep four, it
also doubled as a castle, hideout, ship, and cabin. Austin and
his Grandpa Crosby had painted the interior so it was bright
and clean. We laid down a remnant of Berber carpet so it was
cozy and comfortable. We salvaged the cushions from an old
couch and love seat and put them in the playhouse for chairs
and beds. It was the ideal get-away for the kids. They ate lunch
out there, decorated it at Christmastime, and conducted secret
meetings in it. No adults allowed.

After Austin and his friend had sliced up a bunch of
grapefruits from our tree and thrown them into the neighbor's

yard from the playhouse, I went with him to clean up the mess. We had asked permission to be in Mr. Statler's backyard, but we were out there so long, he came out to see what was going on. I apologized again for the mess and my son's foolishness. He shrugged it off and started telling us a story that began with the famous line, "When I was your age . . ."

The story was amusing initially. However, he got more explicit about how he and his buddies would light couch cushions on fire and throw them up to the ceiling. The non-flammable material turned into super-glue and the cushions would stick to the roof. Remembering the cushions in the playhouse, and knowing Austin's ability to re-enact any scene, I began making hand signals to Mr. Statler to stop the story. He kept chuckling and eventually stopped. Thank goodness.

My children concoct enough harebrained schemes of their own without the help of well-meaning neighbors. God tells us over and over how and why children need proper instruction. First Corinthians 13:11 states, "When I was a child, I talked like a child, I thought like a child, I reasoned like a child." Proverbs 22:15 begins, "Folly is bound up in the heart of a child."

As we discover foolishness in our children, we need to draw it to their attention and explain the outcome. I love Deuteronomy 6:7. God instructs us to teach our children His commandments: "Impress them on your children. Talk about them when you sit at home and when you walk along the road, when you lie down and when you get up." Basically, always!

Our Little Peepers

Since we wouldn't allow our daughter to keep a wild bird that she had caught, Larisa and her brothers started pecking at us to buy some domesticated birds . . . meaning chickens. My mistake? Going to look at the fluffy, little chickies in the feed store.

Being experienced animal keepers, my children checked books out of the library on building coops, raising layers and feeding hens. Rick and I were goners when they presented us a cost analysis showing that it would save us money to have chickens laying eggs for our family to consume.

Thelma, Misty, and Kung Pao were the chosen names for our peeping balls of fluff. We started our babies in a box in the kitchen and discovered the first night at 1:00 A.M. that chicks are quiet only if they are listening to Christian radio.

After a week of being chicken owners, we were going to house-sit for my parents. It wouldn't have been a problem for most grandmas, but my mother was raised sipping tea from English china when she wasn't ironing her bed sheets or arranging fresh flowers in crystal vases. She regularly bleached the grout on her tile countertops. Once we found her ironing her shoe laces. Her home was not exactly chicken-friendly.

We didn't tell Dad and Mom that we were bringing Thelma, Misty and Kung Pao to live in their laundry room. The information sort of slipped out during a phone call while they were away. There was an ant invasion and I called Dad to find out where he kept the bug spray. Jokingly I remarked that his dirty ants were getting on my clean chickens. Oops!

All was fine until the day Kung Pao went missing. I envisioned chicken poop on wool rugs and scratch marks on silk pillows. The half-hour search halted when we discovered that Keeve had taken out Kung Pao so she could go for a ride in the toy train. How thoughtful! Kung Pao was probably bored in her box. A train ride would be an eventful outing for a chicken.

Breathing was a little easier for me when I had all my chicks gathered under "my wings" in the laundry room. It reminded me of the lost lamb that the shepherd went looking for, and how the Lord brings us into His fold. "We all, like sheep, have gone astray" (Isaiah 53:6). Praise the Lord for being our constant Shepherd, drawing us in when we go out for a joy ride.

Family Traditions

If my people, who are called by my name, will humble themselves and pray and seek my face and turn from their wicked ways, then will I hear from heaven and will forgive their sin and will heal their land. Now my eyes will be open and my ears attentive to the prayers offered in this place.

2 Chronicles 7:14,15

Have you heard the story about the woman who always cut the ends off her ham before baking it? Her husband asked her why and she answered, "Because my mother did." Her mother gave the same answer. But the grandmother solved the mystery: "I cut off the ends so it would fit into my roasting pan." Family traditions are peculiar things.

"Go sit on your bed right now and I don't want to hear a peep out of you!" It's not even out of my mouth before I have a flashback to my childhood. I think my mother created that sentence . . . or was it her mother?

Through extensive research, I discovered that this phrase may have come from Old Testament days. Psalm 4:4b reads: "When you are on your beds, search your hearts and be silent." Aha! It was King David's mother who first uttered those immortal words. And it sounded more like, "Blessed child, inheritor of thy father's camels, place thyself reverently on thy resting place, search thy heart and remain in solitude."

It still translates to the same meaning however: "Leave my sight before your constant noise provokes me to wrath." Am I not getting the proper rest? Enough vitamins? Why are the kids pushing all of my buttons? I thought God wouldn't give us more than we can handle? God is the giver of *all* good gifts and He did give us our kids.

I searched the Bible in vain for the verse about children provoking their *parents* to wrath. I've been meaning to write my own version of the Bible. I could include the child-provoking parents verse along with some of my other favorite sayings that God forgot to inspire. For instance, "If Momma ain't happy, ain't nobody happy." Or "I brought you into this world and I can take you out." Is that the absolute truth, or what?

What will my kids remember about home when they are grown and gone? Will it be happy thoughts or memories of a mother gone wild? Our window of opportunity to influence these children will be over before we get our ducks in a row. We need to pray for wisdom. Pray. Pray. Pray.

I need your wisdom, Lord, and guidance once more. I don't want to pray for patience, but it seems like I'm lacking in that area too. Shape and mold my heart to be more like You, patient and caring. Thank You, Lord Jesus. Amen.

CREDIT CARD FRAUD

> *Do not withhold good from those who deserve it, when it is in your power to act. Do not say to your neighbor, "Come back later; I'll give it tomorrow"—when you now have it with you. Do not plot harm against your neighbor, who lives trustfully near you. Do not accuse a man for no reason—when he has done you no harm. Do not envy a violent man or choose any of his ways, for the LORD detests a perverse man but takes the upright into his confidence. The Lord's curse is on the house of the wicked, but he blesses the home of the righteous.*
>
> Proverbs 3:27-33

One Monday morning I received a phone call from my friend Cami. She was doing laundry and discovered a Visa credit card in her son's pocket with my mother's name on it. Unusual, to be sure. All assumptions pointed at my son who is in the same Sunday School class with Cami's boy. Thankfully Cami found the card and called me. She is one of the very few people at our church who knew my mom's name.

At that time, our family was house-sitting at my parent's home while they were on vacation. We had our three children sleeping in separate rooms; Austin slept on the daybed in Grandpa's office. I remembered seeing a stack of credit cards on the top shelf of Dad's desk, so I went to look at them. I didn't know for sure how many were originally there, but the whole pile was gone!

An inquisition was conducted, which produced interesting information from my son's lips. He found cards on Grandpa's desk, which he thought were driver's licenses, so he gave them to his friends at church. What a kind and thoughtful friend, wanting his buddies to be licensed to drive motor vehicles at the age of five.

These were credit cards that my parents received in the mail, but weren't using and hadn't signed. This was a concern for me that I voiced to my husband in front of our generous son. Austin reassured me that he took care of the blank strips by signing all of them himself. Perfect.

I guess the handing out of driver's licenses was a group activity because the only child who could read recounted to his mother a list of the cards and who had them. I spent the remainder of my Monday morning calling all of the parents of the boys in the kindergarten class. Many mothers had indeed found Sears, Home Depot, MasterCard and J.C. Penney charge cards in their boys' possession, but didn't recognize the name of the owner. I collected the cards the following Sunday.

Luke 6:31, which states, "Do to others as you would like them to do to you," was certainly Austin's motto. Pleasure would have been written all over his face if someone gave him a driver's license. He desired for others to feel that pleasure. Sharing is a good thing. But sharing Grandpa's credit cards is not. Did I forget to tell my children the itty-bitty fact that sharing from the heart involves only your own possessions? Parenting is all about the details, isn't it? The important details are the ones I seem to keep missing.

THE HOCKEY MISHAP

> *A truthful witness gives honest testimony, but a false witness tells lies. Reckless words pierce like a sword, but the tongue of the wise brings healing. Truthful lips endure forever, but a lying tongue lasts only a moment. . . . The LORD detests lying lips, but he delights in men who are truthful.*
>
> Proverbs 12:17-19, 22

It was a typical mid-week church night at our home. My husband was working late, leaving me scrambling to get dinner prepared, the kids bathed, and to church on time. I was diligently working toward our departure time when my dripping son entered the kitchen wearing a towel and clutching a bloodstained washcloth to his chin.

On the family emergency scale of one to ten, I quickly ascertained that this was a two: minimal blood, no crying, and a coherently talking child. Austin relayed the story of standing up in the water, slipping and catching his chin on the edge of the tub. I assumed a Snoopy Band-Aid was the answer and we would be only slightly late for service.

Then I looked at the laceration. It would require repeated Snoopy Band-Aids and it escalated to a four on the family emergency scale. I told Austin to get dressed and we would wait to see if the bleeding stopped. He did and it didn't.

"Everyone get in the van. We're going to the hospital," I instructed, impressing even myself with a calm voice. I'd had enough past experience to know that the procedure would be a routine stitch job.

While we waited, a male nurse inquired if Austin played sports. "Yes, hockey," he proudly replied. Then he asked about the cut and Austin related the bathtub wipeout. The nurse proceeded to inform Austin that to save himself some embarrassment he shouldn't tell anyone that he slipped in the tub. He should say there was a hockey mishap. I chuckled. With the sewing complete, we were on our way home.

Austin later told me, "I can't tell anyone this was a hockey cut. That would be lying!" The fear of the Lord was shining forth in my son's life and it did my heart good. Psalm 34:11-13 reads, "Come, my children, listen to me; I will teach you the fear of the LORD. Whoever of you loves life and desires to see many good days, keep your tongue from evil and your lips from speaking lies." Austin had learned enough about telling the truth to know lying when he heard it. The world is quick to "embellish a story" or "improve the truth" but it all boils down to speaking lies. Speak the truth and impart to your children a desire to fear the Lord and see many good days.

Monster Mud Milkshakes

> *The LORD said to Moses: "If anyone sins and is unfaithful to the LORD by deceiving his neighbor about something entrusted to him or left in his care or stolen, or if he cheats him . . . when he thus sins and becomes guilty, he must return what he has stolen or taken by extortion, or what was entrusted to him . . . He must make restitution in full, add a fifth of the value to it and give it all to the owner."*
>
> Leviticus 6:1,2, 4,5

After a Sunday morning service, we rendezvoused at a local Mexican restaurant with friends from a neighboring church. The four of us adults conversed at one end of the table while munching on tortilla chips slathered in salsa, catching up on all of the latest news.

"May I take your order?" interrupted the waiter. There were tacos, taquitos, burritos, tamales, nachos . . . and not a decision made among us, so we sent him down to take the childrens' orders while we tried to stay focused on the task at hand. After making our requests, we started gabbing again and eventually noticed something out of place among our kids. They were all guzzling Monster Mud Milkshakes consisting of crushed Oreo cookies, ice cream, and gummy worms on the surface of the "dirt." Each colossal beverage cost more than an entire kiddy menu meal with pop and dessert! We were quite unimpressed at the audacity of our little bambinos and at ourselves for overlooking their escapades.

Our goal as parents is to raise responsible citizens who are aware of their own actions and of the consequences for stepping over "the line." Monster Mud Milkshakes ordered without permission was stepping over the line. It was apparent from the guilty looks on their faces that they already had knowledge of that fact.

After profuse apologies by the children, their father explained that they would be paying for their sins by picking up olives in our yard. We have six olive trees that generously drop purple, staining fruit. For each yogurt cup filled with olives, they would be rewarded with ten cents.

Guidelines for restitution can be found in Leviticus 6:4,5 where it says that one must return in full what was taken and add a fifth of the value to it. Only 48 cups were needed to make restitution for each four-dollar mud shake ordered.

In her opinion, olive picking was a bit beneath our eldest daughter. So instead of staining her fingers with manual labor she went to her cash stash and took out $4.80. "Here's your money," she announced as she reluctantly presented it to her father. "I'll never order that again without asking, but they sure were good!"

It is important that a child recognizes their sin and repent. Equally significant is the process of asking for forgiveness and performing restitution, even if it has to be purple-handed restitution.

Sticks and Stones Hurt and so do Names

> *The nations will see your righteousness, and all kings your glory; you will be called by a new name that the mouth of the LORD will bestow. You will be a crown of splendor in the LORD's hand, a royal diadem in the hand of your God.*
>
> Isaiah 62:2,3

Proverbs 6:6 was the first verse my son Austin could read. He loves that verse. "Go to the ant, you sluggard; consider its ways and be wise." It is underlined in his Bible and he reads Proverbs often because the ant can be found there. I taught this verse to my kids when they were struggling with building a work ethic.

My husband's brother, Terry, is my favorite example of not wanting a sluggish label. Their mom and maternal grandparents are Cree Indians who lived in the bush in Northern Quebec. When the boys were young, they would spend summers with their people fishing, hunting moose, snaring rabbits, and skinning beavers. They faithfully hauled water, chopped wood, and picked blueberries. Somehow Rick got the Cree name Inu (pronounced EE-new), which translates to Indian or hard worker. Terry received the name In-sti-goo-shoo meaning white man or lazy. (I was given the name Instigooshoo Squish, which they tell me means white girl. I've wondered where the lazy part went, but that's for another time.)

Through the years Terry took much ribbing from family about being the white man who didn't work as hard as the Indians. The "ant" in Terry arose, however, when he and his wife, Jennie, took in three kids and he became Mr. Mom. Terry worked as hard as any stay-at-home-mom—maybe harder because it didn't come naturally to him to cook, clean, wash clothes, make lunches, fold clothes, and talk on the phone simultaneously. In our eyes, he had earned the Inu name. He was no sluggard. Proverbs 6:6 could have been rewritten to, "Go to Terry, you sluggard. Consider his ways and be wise."

However, years of being called Instigooshoo didn't rest easy with Terry. One summer he announced that the Cree Games would be held in Quebec to determine who was the real Inu of the family. Rick and Terry spent a week up in the bush shooting ducks, chewing birch bark, chopping wood, and calling moose. When the chips fell, there were two hardworking Indians. Terry was given the new name Naw-ja-way. We're not sure of the true translation, but Terry thinks it means "Works harder than Inu."

Children don't want to be labeled as lazy or a sluggard. Offer your children uplifting words. "Great job, Champ!" "You're sure a hard worker." "You showed great determination finishing that project!" Then sit back and watch them beam.

THE Free Junk game

These twelve Jesus sent out with the following instructions: "Do not go among the Gentiles or enter any town of the Samaritans. Go rather to the lost sheep of Israel. As you go, preach this message: 'The kingdom of heaven is near.' Heal the sick, raise the dead, cleanse those who have leprosy, drive out demons. Freely you have received, freely give."

Matthew 10:5-8

Call us crazy, but the Crosby's *love* to take road trips. Mention a trip and our eyes sparkle with the anticipation of a visit to AAA for maps and travel guides. Over the years we have listened to numerous books-on-tape, sung every repetitive song known to man, and most importantly played new and exciting vacation games.

It was 2004 when we discovered the favorite travel game of all time: The Free Junk Game. At the outset of a three-day drive from Phoenix to Lake Tahoe, each child was handed a large Ziploc bag and the rules were announced:

1. At each stop, collect free junk.

2. Keep your junk a secret.

3.   No picking garbage off the ground or out of the trash.

4.   Free junk has to be collected from inside an establishment.

After listening attentively, Rick asked for a Ziploc bag. Originally this was a game for the kids, but as I handed Rick his very own Ziploc, my competitive spirit arose and I slipped another into my purse.

All day five Crosby's exited the van on search and destroy missions. Coffee lids, stir sticks, lotto cards, and car-wash advertisements were stealthily stuffed into plastic bags. We looked like a troop of shoplifters making a run on Chevron.

That night we displayed our piles of "free junk" on a hotel bed and proudly held up each item. Identical items were cancelled out and thrown into the trash. It was only the unique junk that earned a point. We tallied and pronounced the first victor, Rick.

With the tough competition of Day 1, the quest heightened for the oddest scrap. That night much glory was taken in the display of a handmade "Out of Order" sign, an application for employment at McDonalds, and my personal collection of six distinctive toilet seat covers. Despite my efforts, my son Austin was the King of Free Junk that night.

Since the commencement of the Free Junk Game, not a trip goes by without secret bags of treasures hidden in our van.

When Jesus sent out the twelve disciples he told them, "Freely you have received, freely give" (Matthew 10:8b). The Free Junk Game can be a great discussion starter for this foundational truth. We have all been offered salvation through Jesus Christ, but was it free? No, Jesus paid the price so we could freely receive. How can we freely give what we have received?

Another Day in Paradise

> *And we urge you, brothers, warn those who are idle, encourage the timid, help the weak, be patient with everyone. Make sure that nobody pays back wrong for wrong, but always try to be kind to each other and to everyone else. Be joyful always; pray continually; give thanks in all circumstances, for this is God's will for you in Christ Jesus.*
>
> 1 Thessalonians 5:14-19

My sinuses were giving me grief and the bright sunlight hurt my eyes. I didn't want to leave the house, but motherly duty called. My hubby had unfortunately rear-ended someone, so we were down to one car. I borrowed my brother's truck to take my daughter to her drama class.

There was a short parent meeting at the beginning of class, so I asked Austin and Keeve if they could handle playing on the playground unsupervised. They said yes. I wasn't convinced. I rattled off a list of restrictions including, "Leave the rocks on the ground. Stay in the playground." They both nodded then ran like the wind toward the teeter-totter.

We learned somewhere along our parenting journey that children visualize your instructions. If you instruct them, "Don't throw rocks," they picture themselves throwing rocks. It was quite a challenge rewording corrective sentences to the positive tense, but I sincerely believe it has improved their behavior.

Anyway, the meeting ended and I walked toward the playground. There I witnessed my sons, both ghostly white from head to toe, beating a five-foot-long Styrofoam pool noodle into a pile of line chalk from the nearby soccer field. They were having the time of their lives! Enter Mom. "Get over here NOW!" It drives me nuts when they giggle as I correct them. It took ten minutes of wet-paper-towel-wiping to clean them up.

Trying to be appreciative of my brother's kindness, I stopped to fill up the truck. I hopped out and gassed up as quickly as possible. When I tried to get back in the truck, I realized the boys had locked me out, a life-threatening move on their part. One fierce glare in the window and the lock clicked open. I silently climbed in and searched for my keys, to no avail. "Where are my keys?" I finally asked exasperated. Then the unthinkable occurred, they broke into hysterical laughter. They had hidden my keys. To their benefit, I have thirty-something years under my belt of listening to sermons on Christ like behavior. If I were still in elementary school, I would have pounded both of them and enjoyed every minute of it.

Proverbs 24:10 says, "If you falter in times of trouble, how small is your strength." Thankfully, "the joy of the LORD is [my] strength" (Nehemiah 8:10c). We need God's strength and joy to be moms—or our children might not live to see their teens.

Effectual Fervent Prayer

> *Rejoice in the Lord always. I will say it again: Rejoice!*
> *Let your gentleness be evident to all. The Lord is near.*
> *Do not be anxious about anything, but in everything by*
> *prayer and petition, with thanksgiving, present your*
> *requests to God. And the peace of God, which transcends*
> *all understanding, will guard your hearts and your*
> *minds in Christ Jesus.*
>
> Philippians 4:4-7

Dogs never appealed to me *at all*. As a mother of three young children, I considered a dog a nuisance that would be added to my collection of little beings that drooled, pooped, and needed to be fed, bathed, and loved. I no more wanted a dog than a triple root canal without Novocain.

To my daughter, caring for her very own puppy was as close to heaven on earth as she could imagine. We were not a good pair. The first time she asked if she could get a dog I responded, "Yes, the day after my funeral." I was serious.

My doggie dogma didn't deter Larisa. She pleaded her case to her father. Knowing my aversion to dogs, he wisely discerned that a miracle was her only hope. His invaluable advice: "Ask God to change your mother's heart." Thus began the nightly bedtime prayer ritual of her earnestly requesting, "God, please change my mother's heart so I can have a dog." I about choked the first time I heard how sincere she was. It saddened my heart that her dream was unattainable.

Night after night she laid her request before the Lord. After six months I thought she would relent and assume God wasn't listening. Not so. I soon discovered that every Sunday in Children's Church at prayer request time, Larisa would faithfully raise her hand and ask fellow prayer warriors to pray that God would change her mother's heart so she could get a dog. Months later I noticed a card with familiar handwriting posted on the church's prayer wall, asking others to join the onslaught against me. What was she thinking? I was born hating dogs. My mother hated dogs.

Nine months passed and her vigil continued. A year slipped by and her hand was continually shooting heavenward in Children's Church. Church workers began interrogating me to see if God was changing my heart. I felt like kicking them in the shins. Somewhere between 17 and 18 months . . . something remarkable occurred. Teeny weenie doggie faces began appealing to me. At least large-eyed, floppy-eared puppies did. At the two-year mark, I asked my husband if we could get a puppy for Larisa. The only explanation is that God answers prayer.

Larisa's life mirrored James 5:16c: "The effectual fervent prayer of a righteous man [or girl!] availeth much." Next time you're in Arizona, stop by and meet Trixie. She's *our* dog. I have since discovered three things we can learn from a dog:

1. Be loyal.

2. When loved ones come home, always run to greet them.

3. When you're happy, dance around, and wag your entire body.

Parallels from the Preeners

Make my joy complete by being likeminded, having the
same love, being one in spirit and purpose. Do nothing
out of selfish ambition or vain conceit, but in humility
consider others better than yourselves. Each of you
should look not only to your own interests, but also to
the interests of others. Your attitude should be the same
as that of Christ Jesus.

Philippians 2:2-5

If our three chickens were pecking and scratching in Jesus'
time, I'm sure He would have used them in a parable about
mothers.

Misty was the largest of the three roost mates. She was a
beautiful Americana with colorful feathers that laid dazzling
green eggs. She strutted around the yard like a rooster, looking
exquisite as the sun brought out the yellows, reds, and greens
in her plumage. Misty acted brave, but she was really a scaredy-
cat. She would run and hide from humans, dogs and remote-
controlled cars.

Misty reminded me of a mom who looks good on the outside,
all made-up and put together. Matching shoes and purse.
Manicured and pedicured. The facade disguises fear, insecurity,
and a need to please.

Thelma was a skinny Blue Andalusian who was pure white with two shimmering blue spots on her head. She was wiry from the get go. She's the only one of our chickens that ever pecked anyone. And could she run! Thelma was hard to catch and out of control. She laid small white eggs with thick shells.

Thelma symbolized the uptight type-A woman who seems to be running in four directions at once. She is a no-nonsense mom who wears a ponytail for immediate departures. She's frazzled and overcommitted. She can't remember the last time she sat down to relax and Starbucks is her source.

Kung Pao personified the cute baby chick: fluffy and fun. She grew to be a chubby brown Rhode Island Red, a faithful layer and a friendly playmate for my son Keeve. He carried her under one arm and included her in all his games. She rode on the handle bars of his bike and inside his mini grocery cart. Kung Pao sat next to Keeve in the Power-Wheels Jeep relishing the wind in her feathers. Surprisingly, she was the bravest and meanest bird when any animal attacked the chickens. She was fierce and would peck till blood flowed to protect her sisters.

Kung Pao was the epitome of a productive, faithful, and loving mother. This mother could let her hair down and howl with the kids. She is ordinary in appearance, yet clean and tidy. She is the mom who loyally makes real dinners with fresh food. She's the neighborhood Kool-Aid mom. But hurt her kids and you'll be facing terror of the worst kind. This is the mother that I aim to be—dependable, leaning on the Lord for strength and genuinely complete.

LET MOMMA TESTIFY!

> *From everlasting to everlasting the LORD's love is with those who fear him, and his righteousness with their children's children—with those who keep his covenant and remember to obey his precepts.*
>
> Psalm 103:17,18

The Lord has blessed me with several bosom friends, yet none invited me to the Sisters Rodeo until I met Jill, the cowgirl from Silverton, Oregon. This barrel-riding filly is cleverly disguised as an urban housewife until you visit her home, which is tastefully decorated in cowboy pictures and lassoes.

Bosom friends go to events like The Biggest Little Show in the World because we care about what makes our soul-sister tick. We are genuinely interested in where each other came from, where we went to school, and who the family is that shaped our lives. Bosom friends love our kids nearly as much as we do. They feed our dog when we go on vacation. Mostly, they understand us and love us anyway.

Before leaving for the shindig, I discovered that we would be traveling right by the resting place of some of my relatives. Shedd-Pugh Cemetery is a grassy clearing surrounded by towering pines in Linn County, Oregon. Jill was more than willing to spend some time trudging over the mushy grass to help me locate the marble epitaph of Mercer and Sarah Thompson, my great-great grandparents who crossed the Oregon Trail and started the Methodist Church in Oregon. She even grabbed a stick, assisted in the moss-removal and the general tending of the 118-year-old gravesite.

That day was awesome, not just because I was with a bosom friend or because we found the tombstone, but because I had one of those sacred "God moments." Standing in the cool breeze taking in the experience, I realized the people buried there had most likely prayed for me. They were my family. My ancestry.

Sometimes those of us who have been saved since we were young don't think we have a testimony. What a lie! It's an awesome testament to the Lord's faithfulness that He protected and flourished a family of believers through many generations. Revelation 12:11 tells us that we overcome the devil "by the blood of the Lamb and by the word of [our] testimony." In order to overcome Satan we need to tell others of the Lord's goodness, His love, and His sacrifice. There is power in our words!

If you came from a family rich in Christian heritage as I have, rejoice! Share it with others. If not, then you are the one whom God chose to start the rich heritage of prayer and solid faith for your family generations to come.

HiT Me WiTH your BesT SHOT

> *As a prisoner for the Lord, then, I urge you to live a life worthy of the calling you have received. Be completely humble and gentle; be patient, bearing with one another in love. Make every effort to keep the unity of the Spirit through the bond of peace.*
>
> Ephesians 4:1-3

Hockey is the national sport of Canada. Most of our family is from Canada, so hockey is the national sport of the Crosby's, no matter where we live. You would think a hockey league for kids would be non-existent in Arizona, but alas, my husband located several.

The team our boys were on this season was lacking a goalie, so our youngest son decided to play goal. At six, Keeve is as wide as he is tall in the goalie equipment. Conveniently for retrieving pucks, he fit under the crossbar when standing straight up in skates. Keeve had a lot to learn since this was his first experience playing this position.

Watching the opposing team's score rise with every other shot on Keeve was almost more than I could handle. His first game was spent getting used to wearing all the padding and looking like the Michelin Man. During the second game, Keeve mastered the skill of skating from post to post in the net. The third game introduced the poke check and stacking the pads. Finally, during his fourth game, he figured out how to block shots! What a glorious day!

Rick and I were extremely proud of Keeve's determination to play goal and his ability to persevere when player after player kept scoring on him. It was the fifth game, incidentally, when Keeve started yelling. From my seat behind the glass I couldn't make out what he was saying. Numerous times Keeve's voice could be heard in the arena, but I didn't know what he was saying until after the game. When asked, he grinned and repeated, "Come on! Give me your best shot!" Here he was a six-year-old, playing with seven- and eight-year-olds who could score on him at will, acting cocky and enticing his opponents.

Keeve's self-assuredness combined with lack of experience shamefully compared to my life in many areas. How many times have I been prideful after my first feeble attempts at something? Completing the first two lessons in a 12-week Bible study on Ephesians brought out, "Sure, I've studied Paul's letter to the church at Ephesus." Oh brother! Who was I trying to impress? Fortunately I pursued the study further and discovered an interesting verse in Ephesians 4:2: "Be completely humble and gentle." Oh boy. I should have read all of Ephesians before pronouncing my vast knowledge . . . without humility or gentleness.

CODE NINE IN THE PETTING ZOO

> *After three days they found [Jesus] in the temple courts... When his parents saw him, they were astonished. His mother said to him, "Son, why have you treated us like this? Your father and I have been anxiously searching for you." "Why were you searching for me?" he asked. "Didn't you know I had to be in my Father's house?" But they did not understand what he was saying to them. Then he went down to Nazareth with them and was obedient to them. But his mother treasured all these things in her heart.*
>
> Luke 2:46, 48-51

My sister and her family were visiting from Washington, so we planned a family outing to the Phoenix Zoo. The pungent smell of animals hung in the air, as we consumed our lunch on the grassy bank beside the fountains of the man-made lake. After the food was devoured, our flock headed down the pathway past Monkey Island to Harmony Farm Petting Zoo.

With six adults, nine children and two strollers we moved like a herd of elephants, loud and lumbering. The huge, red barn welcomed us as a cool oasis from the sun. Half of our pack went through the double gates to attack the goats with the provided hairbrushes. The fraidy-cat half played it safe and took photos from the far side of the fence.

My attention was following my nephew's attempts at brushing a pesky horned goat when I noticed that my two boys were not in sight. I scanned the petting zoo and the surrounding areas. No boys. I questioned my family members, but no one remembered when Austin and Keeve were last with us. Immediately I asked the Lord if the boys were in danger. A peace washed over me and I knew my guys were safe, but going to be very sorry when they were found.

Eventually an inquiry with zoo personnel located my sons back at the fountains where we had eaten lunch. The boys were brought to me in a golf cart, looking terribly sheepish, but holding up a brave front. After the initial hugs and kisses I cross-examined the boys, which brought on shaky voices, wobbly lips and brimming eyes.

"Why have you done this? We have been anxiously searching for you." Those were my words, but they were also Mary's words when Jesus was found in the temple courts after three days of searching. The fact that Mary once lost Jesus gave me hope. Even the mother God chose for His only Son was capable of losing her boy . . . for *three* days. Hello! Austin and Keeve will turn out exactly how God has planned despite my sometimes bumbling efforts as their mother.

The glimpses of Jesus as a boy from the New Testament provide comfort for those of us raising boys. Pray often over your boys that they will grow "in wisdom and stature, and in favor with God and men" just like Jesus did (see Luke 2:52).

Escalator Escapades

Shopping usually isn't harmful to your health, unless the Lord is trying to use you as an example to your children.

I was riding up the department store escalator with my 11-year-old daughter, Larisa, when she gave me a hair-raising report of her father and brothers from that exact store. Apparently my husband, who is simply a ten-year-old boy trapped in an aging body, offered one of his sons $2.00 to run up the descending escalator. I held my breath waiting for the outcome. Disappointed, I learned of the mad dash, the laughter, and the payoff.

Proverbs 12:15 came to mind: "The way of a fool seems right to him, but a wise man listens to advice." Mentally I lumped the females in my family on the wise side and the males on the foolish side. Being a lover of safety regulations, I painstakingly cautioned Larisa why it was so foolish to run up the escalator.

"You could hurt yourself and others, possibly even an elderly person."

With the hour-and-a-half long task of picking out blinds completed, we were on our way back toward the escalator. Just as our feet touched the top stair, I remembered beautifully decorated black towels calling my name on the floor we were leaving. Disregarding every word I had spoken 90 minutes previously, I told my daughter to turn around and run back up the few steps that had descended. Obediently she turned and ran, safely disembarking three feet from where I landed—face down, kissing the metal platform, half on and half dangling down the mobile staircase.

Escalators should have automatic shut-off systems built in them in case someone like me falls while riding. Obviously, this one didn't and since the lower half of my body was on moving ground, my knees were taking quite a beating with each consecutive step that the metal monster spit out. With upper body strength that I wasn't aware I possessed, I pulled my lower half to safety and slowly stood to analyze the damage. Blood trickled from my big toe, but other than some up-and-coming bruises, I didn't look too beat up.

To our surprise and relief, there were no witnesses to the way of a fool that seemed right to me. Momentarily I visited the foolish side of the family, but thankfully I'm back on the wise side and my plans are to stay there.

Adding disappointment to injury, the towels were MIA, and my daughter confirmed, "You were right, Mom! That was not safe!"

OUT OF THE MOUTHS OF BABES

> "Are you still so dull?" Jesus asked them. "Don't you see that whatever enters the mouth goes into the stomach and then out of the body? But the things that come out of the mouth come from the heart, and these make a man 'unclean.' For out of the heart come evil thoughts, murder, adultery, sexual immorality, theft, false testimony, slander. These are what make a man 'unclean'; but eating with unwashed hands does not make him 'unclean.'"
>
> Matthew 15:16-20

Neither Larisa nor Austin put non-edible items in their mouths. When witnessing another child eating rocks, chewing dog toys, or licking the windows in the car, I assumed the parent was not parenting very well. Isn't it easy to pick out what other parents need to work on? Certainly I was the better parent, in my humble opinion, because my children didn't gnaw on the unsanitary grocery cart handle. Eeeewwww!

Then in 1998 I gave birth to Keeve Kennedy Crosby. Without my knowledge, I crossed over into the lump of parents who couldn't stop their little beavers from chewing the crib apart. When Keeve started crawling Lego's had to be hidden and Barbie shoes needed a safe haven. Keeve put anything and everything into his mouth: lint, keys, jewelry (while I was wearing it!), washcloths, even toilet paper.

While changing Keeve's messy diaper one day, what to my wondering eyes should appear, but seven colorful plastic flowers from the Play Mobil set. Well, at least that proved Keeve's digestive system was fully functioning.

Chuck E. Cheese brought on our biggest scare by supplying three-year-old Keeve with a game token. I was passing by our hall bathroom and heard muffled gurgling noises. Upon glancing in, I saw my baby boy unable to breathe, turning pasty white . . . choking. One swift Heimlich maneuver and the token popped out on the bathmat. Hopefully, I thought that would be the close call that would stop his dangerous habit.

Not so. Keeve is approaching his seventh birthday, but alas, every single day I hear myself ask, "What is in your mouth? Throw it away." Unbelievable. He has consumed museum brochures in their entirety, chewed driftwood for over 500 miles, and slowly digested 50% of his plastic hockey mouth guard. "It's building his immunities," I quip to vindicate myself.

Keeve came to mind when I read Matthew 15:11 where Jesus said, "What goes into a man's mouth does not make him 'unclean,' but what comes out of his mouth, that is what makes him 'unclean.'" What we speak comes from our hearts. If we dwell on issues that keep us angry, unsatisfied and jealous, the words out of our mouths will be unclean. What we put in is what comes out. If we desire to have our children speak words of righteousness and truth, we need to plant God's Word in the fertile soil of their hearts.

scorpions, rattlers and coyotes, oh my!

> *No widow may be put on the list of widows unless she is over sixty, has been faithful to her husband, and is well known for her good deeds, such as bringing up children, showing hospitality, washing the feet of the saints, helping those in trouble and devoting herself to all kinds of good deeds.*
>
> 1 Timothy 5:9,10

First Timothy 5:9,10 gives a list of good deeds that women should practice if they are to qualify as true "New Testament" widows. The verses list several good deeds, but the two that caught my eye were "bringing up children" and "showing hospitality." Understandably, the admonishment for bringing up children is in our best interest, since the kids we raise will eventually take care of us. (I realize this may be 50 years from now, but it wasn't raining when Noah built the ark!)

Hospitality, however, must be learned then taught. One of our goals as a family is to use our home to bless others. We recently moved to a new home . . . in a new subdivision . . . in the desert, where we have already begun inviting guests to visit. One would assume that with Phoenix's mild winter temperatures, entertaining would be a delightful outdoor experience. Oh contraire.

"Dinner-then-games" nights are a family favorite, but guests must arrive before dusk in order to avoid the diamondback rattlesnakes that slither on our sidewalks when the sun sinks behind the mountains.

If the family has small children, we warn them not to play by the wood pile since that is where we once found a scorpion the size of a mouse.

When overnight guests bless us with their company, they don't get the common, "Good night, sleep tight" bedtime send-off. Casually we inform them that they might be stirred from their slumber by wild crying and screaming noises from our neighborhood coyote pack. Not to fear; they haven't harmed anyone . . . yet.

No matter where you live or what your situation, you can practice hospitality. Your home is good training ground as kids feel most comfortable in familiar surroundings. Ask them to take coats as guests arrive and to offer to show children the toy room. Children love to feel important. What better way than to ask them to serve others? Kids can ask guests the type of beverage they prefer with dinner. They can serve a tray of cookies or a plate of sliced fruit. They can also clear the table and help with clean-up.

Have a practice night where Dad is treated as a guest, and the kids offer the food and clear the table without the fear of "messing it up" in front of others.

I didn't come up with this on my own. It was God's idea. He told all of us to "practice hospitality" (Romans 12:13b). Remember, where there's smoke, there's dinner.

crazy woman Driver!

> *Remember your Creator in the days of your youth, before the days of trouble come and the years approach when you will say, "I find no pleasure in them"—before the sun and the light and the moon and the stars grow dark, and the clouds return after the rain; when the keepers of the house tremble, and the strong men stoop, when the grinders cease because they are few, and those looking through the windows grow dim.*
>
> Ecclesiastes 12:1-3

The Lord allowed me a mere glimpse into old age this past week. It all started when friends called in the morning to ask if they could pick up some boxes in an hour. I forgot. Yes, in 60 minutes time it completely left my mind. I covered well, even though I had bed-head, mascara under my eyes, and furry teeth.

I promised my sister-in-law, Julie, that I'd watch my nephew during his nap. I forgot and went grocery shopping. I didn't cover well at all that time. I profusely apologized and felt horrible.

Next, I put ground beef in the electric frying pan, turned it on high and then went out to check on the boys in the front yard. Outside, I took my sweet time watering plants. I returned to the smell of burning meat, reminding myself, *Oh yeah! I was cooking!*

As I separated the black from the red meat, two truck loads of men arrived to pour cement in a section of our driveway. I went out to move the car and accidentally backed towards the men and their wheelbarrows . . . twice. I was impressed by how fast they moved out of the way both times.

Ecclesiastes 12 lists some of the calamities that befall the aged. Eyes grow dim. Arms tremble. Hearing fades. Teeth go MIA. Verse one says, "Remember your Creator in the days of your youth, before the days of trouble come." The Lord was very convincing as He allowed me a day of trouble. I wanted to yell at Him, "I'M REMEMBERING YOU! Please give me my brain back!"

After the driveway was poured, I warned the boys to steer clear of the wet cement. Later, my son Austin sheepishly came and told me that he accidentally ran through the setting concrete . . . in his black suede tennis shoes that we had bought the previous day. His reason: He forgot the cement was wet.

I barely stopped myself from screaming, "HOW COULD YOU FORGET?" Great question for the day! How could I forget my friends were coming for boxes? Or forget my promise to watch my nephew? Or sizzling beef on the stove? Or how to back the car out of the driveway?

Maybe it was for my son's sake that I had forgotten a whole handful of things that day. Nobody got mad at me when I forgot time and time again. (O.K., maybe the cement guys did.) God is so timely in giving us experiences that parallel our childrens' accidents. I believe He does it so we don't blow a gasket when they slip up.

making a Deposit in the offering plate

> "Bring the whole tithe into the storehouse, that there
> may be food in my house. Test me in this," says the LORD
> Almighty, "and see if I will not throw open the floodgates
> of heaven and pour out so much blessing that you will
> not have room enough for it."
>
> Malachi 3:10

Rick and I were worshipfully listening to the offertory on a Sunday morning when Diane appeared in the aisle beside us. Diane is an angel who works in the children's department and her sudden appearance was as startling to me as the angels who scared the shepherds on the night of Jesus' birth. She was, however, not bringing good tidings of great joy. Kneeling beside us she spoke in a hushed voice, "When the offering bucket was passed, your son spit in it." Certainly not tidings of comfort and joy. We thanked her for alerting us and confirmed that we would chasten the boy.

Later, sitting on my bed with my son, the spitter, I asked if he knew what spitting meant. "No," he whispered. "It's bad. Really bad," I sternly responded. Opening my Bible, I read aloud from Matthew 27:27, 30-31: "Then the governor's soldiers took Jesus into the Praetorium and gathered the whole company of soldiers around him . . . They spit on him, and took the staff and struck him on the head again and again. After they had mocked him, they . . . led him away to crucify him." My son's face sobered as I explained how evil the soldiers were. They were doing the worst things they could think of to Jesus and spitting was one of them.

Then we discussed how putting money in the offering is giving a gift to Jesus. I questioned him to make sure he understood, "So when the offering bucket came to you and it was your turn to give a gift to Jesus, what did you do?" "I spit like the soldiers," he quietly replied.

It was a good lesson for my son, who will never again spit in the offering plate . . . hopefully. It was also a good lesson for me. I could barely read the passage from Matthew without getting choked up. Those soldiers were cruel to *my* Jesus. He could have stopped them, but He did not . . . for me and my sins. For you and your sins.

He offers his love and forgiveness. But in our selfishness, when we do things our own way, we join the soldiers. When we are struggling in our own strength, we're mocking the Lord's power to assist us. Refusing to allow God to help us is like spitting in the offering plate.

Help me to bring you the offering of my will, Lord. Please keep me in Your will and allow me to accept Your good gifts. Amen.

Lessons from the Lagoon

> *My son, preserve sound judgment and discernment, do not let them out of your sight; they will be life for you, an ornament to grace your neck. Then you will go on your way in safety, and your foot will not stumble; when you lie down, you will not be afraid; when you lie down, your sleep will be sweet.*
>
> Proverbs 3:21-24

Myrtle and George are our Red-Eared Sliders who arrived at our door in a Styrofoam hamburger box. They are tiny turtles about the size of silver dollars. We also ordered their kidney-shaped lagoon complete with a mini, plastic palm tree for their island. Myrtle and George are my kind of pets. They don't take up much room. They are silent. They are very entertaining to play with or simply hold. And they stay put on the kitchen counter . . . well, George does anyway.

Myrtle's escape was discovered one Sunday after church. Plain and simple, she was gone and George wasn't going to be an accomplice. His pointy lips were sealed. (He probably gave her a boost.) We searched the entire kitchen counter, the sink and the disposal without success. I worried about Myrtle's well-being after her apparent jump off the kitchen counter. That would be like me jumping off a 20 story building. Grant it, God did give Myrtle a hard shell.

We hunted throughout the kitchen, pulling out the fridge and stove, and then expanded the search into adjacent rooms. We called in an additional search and rescue team (my brother and niece) and announced a $1.00 reward for the return of Myrtle. The search wasn't called off, but it came to a halt after we'd searched an hour and Myrtle's whereabouts was still a mystery.

My niece and I were chatting in the kitchen when we heard a muffled scratching noise. "Did you hear that?" I asked. "I think it came from the stove!" I pulled out the drawer under the oven and, sure enough, there was Myrtle stuck in a little space by the leg of the stove. It took another 30 minutes, a flashlight, a paintbrush, a screwdriver and sheer will to free Myrtle.

Myrtle and I have a lot in common. If we stay where we are supposed to—in God's will or the lagoon, as the case may be—we are taken care of, fed and safe. It's when we step out of the Lord's will, or the lagoon, that our lives become a series of dangerous situations. We inevitably get ourselves stuck between a rock and a hard place, or stove grooves, and need to be rescued. Myrtle and I both need to stay where the Lord has provided protection and nourishment, in His will and in the lagoon.

How 'bout you? Do you need to learn a lesson from Myrtle the turtle?

TROPHY SHOP JITTERS

> *My flesh and my heart may fail, but God is the strength of my heart and my portion forever. Those who are far from you will perish; you destroy all who are unfaithful to you. But as for me, it is good to be near God. I have made the Sovereign LORD my refuge; I will tell of all your deeds.*
>
> Psalm 73:26-28

The gift of confrontation is not mentioned in the Bible where gifts are listed. I'm not so sure confrontation is actually a gift, but it certainly has been a part of my life several agonizing times.

It was Science Fair 2005 and I was in charge of trophies. Ordering was painless. Picking up was prickly. The engraving shop had made an error by making first, second and third place trophies all blue instead of red, white and blue. The owner of the shop made it out to be my fault for ordering on the phone instead of ordering in person. Aggravated but not wanting to cause grief, I took the blue trophies home.

Two days later at the Science Fair some members of the committee expressed disappointment that the trophies were so similar. As much as I didn't want to, I retraced my steps to the trophy shop. That sort of confrontation makes me highly uncomfortable. I prayed a prayer of desperation to the Lord and went to the shop with my two oldest children. The owner was a loud "I'm-in-charge-here" kind of guy. He was borderline obnoxious when I pointed out his mistake and requested that he make it right. He barked, "Four days." I countered, "Four hours." We stood staring at one another for an eternity it seemed. He was waiting for me to leave with my tail between my legs. My tail was between my legs, but I stood firm. Finally he commanded one of his employees to fix the trophies and stomped off.

Fixing the trophies took five minutes and we were out of there. In the van I mumbled how uncomfortable that type of encounter made me feel. My daughter was surprised and reassured me, "Mom, you sounded so confident!" My tail started to wag again just a wee bit. I confessed that I had prayed before we went in and the Lord gave me boldness.

My children had much to say about Mr. Trophy Shop Owner and how he could improve his people skills and increase business. God planned that trip to the awards store for all of us to learn lessons of reliance on God and business savvy!

Psalm 138:3 reads, "When I called, you answered me; you made me bold and stouthearted." The tri-colored Science Fair trophies were a visual "Amen" to that promise. I wanted to claim one of the trophies as a testament of the Lord making me stouthearted.

WHere's THe orange juice?

> *Do not let any unwholesome talk come out of your mouths, but only what is helpful for building others up according to their needs, that it may benefit those who listen . . . Be kind and compassionate to one another, forgiving each other, just as in Christ God forgave you.*
>
> Ephesians 4:29, 32

There is a line of wisdom in 2 Corinthians 13:7 that should be every parent's prayer. We have offered it up to the Lord upon leaving our children with babysitters and their grandparents. We also pray it when the children are in our own care. It reads, "Now we pray to God that you will not do anything wrong." That's it. That should take care of anything that our children could get into.

Somehow little mishaps still seem to occur in our absence. Like the broken windows, or the paperclips in the computer disc drive, or the white auto paint on the gray dashboard, or the cream-rinse covered dog, or the 31 broken hanger hooks . . . Need I go on? Yes! It's kind of like therapy for me. What about all of Daddy's socks in the toilet, or the gallon of orange juice poured on the couch, or the crayon happy faces that smiled at me from the sliding glass doors, the toy box, the toys, the wall in the hall and our mirrored closet doors?

I stopped reporting these incidences to my mother, as her response was invariably predictable: "Where were you when that was happening?" It was not a question of comfort to me. I felt like saying, "I was in the other room praying to God that they would not do anything wrong."

Upon my return from the hospital after a minor surgery, I arrived home to find my son's name carved backwards into the paint on the oven door. My mother had been watching him when the act was perpetrated. The first question that came to mind for my mother was, "Where were you when that was happening?" But, by God's grace, I held my tongue from criticism and proclaimed with a smile, "Look! That's the first time his S is in the right direction!" My son beamed with pride. Later we had a discussion on the proper care of the home God has given us.

Paul continued on in the same chapter with words that ring true to every parent, "Our prayer is for your perfection . . . that when I come I may not have to be harsh in my use of authority—the authority the Lord gave me for building you up, not for tearing you down." Our parental authority is strictly for building up. Use it wisely!

THE BEST CHRISTMAS PAGEANT EVER

> *And there were shepherds living out in the fields nearby, keeping watch over their flocks at night. An angel of the Lord appeared to them, and the glory of the Lord shone around them, and they were terrified. But the angel said to them, "Do not be afraid. I bring you good news of great joy that will be for all the people. Today in the town of David a Savior has been born to you; he is Christ the Lord. This will be a sign to you: You will find a baby wrapped in cloths and lying in a manger."*
>
> Luke 2:8-12

Wonderful memory-making opportunities exist, especially at Christmas. One year we decided to do a family pageant. There were eight adults, four kids and baby Madison, my niece. Perfect! We put a four-year-old in charge and were amazed at the results. She didn't assign parts, except for the obvious Baby Jesus. She listed the necessary people, divided them into "girl parts" and "boy parts" and we drew out of two stockings for our roles.

My husband drew "wise man" which I thought was appropriate. After all, he married me. Just as suitable, my sister and brother were the other wise guys. Grandpa drew "Joseph." Grandma and my son were shepherds. My sister-in-law was the inn keeper. When my brother-in-law read "donkey," he immediately asked who would be Mary, wondering if a chiropractor would be needed come New Year's Day. To his relief, my 38-pound daughter was Mary. My niece was the angel of the Lord. I was the sheep.

We raided Grandma's closet and found most of our costumes: silky robes, slips and gaudy jewelry. The shepherds wore pillow cases tied with scarves on their heads and wielded hockey sticks for staffs. The donkey wore a brown ski hat and tucked in brown socks for ears. I donned a fluffy white robe and cotton balls in my hair.

It started out as fun, but I was overcome with realization of the truth, starting with the angel of the Lord speaking to Mary from the fireplace hearth. Wearing a white slip and garland in her hair, Whitney stoically quoted from Luke, "Do not be afraid, Mary, you have found favor with God. You will be with child and give birth to a son, and you are to give him the name Jesus. He will be great and will be called the Son of the Most High." Son of the Most High. Wow!

The rest played out with several details that aren't mentioned in the Bible. Baby Jesus cried. Hard. The sheep was obviously unruly, as the shepherd continually used the staff to keep her in line. The Magi strutted in with hokey gifts and we all sang a grand finale, "Glory . . . Glory to God . . . Glory to God in the highest."

Because dramatization is the highest form of learning, acting out stories of faith cements them in our minds. If you want your kids to remember the truth, act it out with them. Our children ask for a repeat performance of the best Christmas pageant every year.

ELVIS HAS LEFT THE BUILDING

> *Then Jesus said to his disciples: "Therefore I tell you, do not worry about your life, what you will eat; or about your body, what you will wear. Life is more than food, and the body more than clothes. Consider the ravens: They do not sow or reap, they have no storeroom or barn; yet God feeds them. And how much more valuable you are than birds!"*
>
> Luke 12:22-24

One of a plethora of pets that have been under the care and keeping of Crosby children was Shelly Elvis Charley Crosby. Each child christened the pet who was simply referred to as Elvis. The purchase of the hermit crab came at a weak moment in my dear husband's life, accompanied by all three children at Paradise Valley Mall. Shelly Elvis Charley was on display in one of those little booths that take up walking room from serious shoppers. The immense purple shell clawing its way across the sand amongst 50 inmates caught the attention of one offspring, and the rest joined in the pursuit of a new pet.

Much preparation had already gone into the acquisition of a hermit crab, but the local pet stores had been out of them for weeks. The home was prepared, complete with a swimming hole and food trough, as well as a broken terracotta pot hideout. But the hermit crabs at the mall were *way* more expensive than the Wal-Mart or Petco counterparts. But alas, Rick succumbed to pee-wee sized peer pressure and purchased Elvis.

My children's first encounter with hermit crabs was at my friend Veronica's house, and they fascinated my zookeepers. I vividly remember Veronica's words of warning, "They never live through molting!"

Fast forward 18 months to Elvis finally molting on our kitchen counter. Indeed the exoskeleton was hollow and Elvis was hiding in a new shell that was caringly placed in his tank for such a time as this. Sadly, I explained to the children that Elvis was most likely dying, but only time would tell.

Two weeks later, after no signs of life, I picked up the shell and peered inside at Elvis. He was dead. Having never seen a hermit crab without his house on his back, I decided a great science lesson would be had by all if I pulled out the dead crab. Surrounded by Larisa, Austin and Keeve, with needle nosed pliers in hand, I proceeded to pull off the main claw of Elvis's corpse. To our horror, it bled, and Elvis cringed. After another two weeks, indeed Veronica's words had proven true. Hermit crabs never live through molting, especially after being pulled apart with pliers.

The moral of the story: Leave God's creatures well enough alone. He designed them to do their business without human intervention. If God wants Elvis to leave the building, he doesn't need our help.

THE DUSTPAN MAN

> *But I call to God, and the Lord saves me. Evening, morning and noon I cry out in distress, and he hears my voice . . . Cast your cares on the Lord and he will sustain you; he will never let the righteous fall.*
>
> Psalm 55:16, 17, 22

Our children were assigned chores as soon as they were capable of carrying objects. Putting trash in the garbage can, taking shoes to the entry closet and collecting scattered toys were ingrained before they could beg for Pop Tarts. As the kids matured and their abilities increased, the chore chart was birthed, and keeping house has been a joint effort ever since. I was determined not to be the maid for my family.

While touring the house on my "who's-hiding-during-chore-time" rounds, my son's reflection on the finger-smudged dining room window caught my attention. Pausing stealthily around the corner, I watched as he swept the entryway. My motherly heart beat proud as he methodically filled the dustpan. I silently congratulated myself: *Another child successfully trained in removing dirt from my tile floors. His wife will profusely thank me some day. He truly has learned a life skill that will serve him well throughout his days. He will rise up and call me blessed.*

Interrupting my thoughts of maternal grandeur, my breath stuck in my throat as I witnessed a horror of horrors. With entryway dirt securely in the dustpan, my son set the broom against the wall, obviously to open the front door for disposal purposes. The door remained untouched, to my grief, as he crossed the living room carpet and gingerly dumped the dirt, sand, rocks, leaves, hair, bugs and lint behind the yellow sofa.

"HEY!" I blasted, a moment too late. In shock his feet left the floor and a derelict grin crossed his used-to-be-darling face. "How long have you been dumping dirt back there?" I demanded.

A pause . . . then, "A while." His honest answer was barely a whisper.

He told the truth . . . one point for his side. After peering behind the couch, I adjusted his score to minus 27. Together we pulled out the couch, vacuumed and went through the rightful motions of putting dirt where dirt belongs.

Through the retraining of my son, the Lord reminded me of the many times I dump the dirt of my life behind the couch instead of dealing with it properly. Psalm 68:19 reassures us that God daily bears our burdens. He is waiting for us to follow the directions in the Bible . . . and bring the sins of our lives to Him.

THE parable OF THE popsicle man

> *If you forgive men when they sin against you, your heavenly Father will also forgive you. But if you do not forgive men their sins, your Father will not forgive your sins . . . Then Peter came to Jesus and asked, "Lord, how many times shall I forgive my brother when he sins against me? Up to seven times?" Jesus answered, "I tell you, not seven times, but seventy-seven times" . . . Forgive your brother from your heart.*
>
> Matthew 6:14,15; 18:21,22, 35b

Children believe what their parents tell them to be absolute truth. It's an unwritten code of parental ethics to lead your offspring in accuracy and truthfulness. It builds trust between the child and the parent. The Lord Almighty admonished Israel to, "Speak the truth to each other" (Zechariah 8:16b).

It's true confession time for Rick and me. We lied to our children about the Popsicle man. We thought it was in our best interest to produce a story regarding his purpose. Hundreds of dollars were safely kept in our billfolds until the naked truth was leaked.

The first time the jingle of the white van danced in Larisa's ears, she asked, "Why does that man drive around and play music?"

Frankly, I should have told the truth, but no, I explained that the man's music was to remind children to love their parents. "All kids are supposed to run and hug their mothers when they hear the music play." I even pointed out the older kids across the street running into their house when the melody came singing into our neighborhood.

Eager to please, Larisa would dash toward me and wrap her little arms around my legs when she heard the Popsicle man's tunes. It was truly heartwarming. Shamefully, the deception went on for several years . . . until we were with a group of families picnicking together. By that time, two of our children were scurrying to us when the shaky speaker serenaded us. As usual, when they heard the song, they hugged us, kissed us and told us they loved us. Then they noticed all the other kids running toward the sticker-covered vehicle and waving green bills in the hot summer air.

"What are they doing?" Larisa asked innocently.

One sad glance passed between her father and me. Then he replied, "They are going to buy popsicles."

"How do they know the music man has popsicles today?"

"He always has them, Sweetheart."

I'll never forget the look of astonishment on Larisa's chubby little face. Norman Rockwell painted it so well in *Discovery,* his depiction of a boy finding a Santa suit in his dad's dresser drawer.

Larisa found our little falsehood genuinely funny. She even trained her youngest brother to run and hug us when the Popsicle man approached. Children are so forgiving. Buy them an ice cream and all is well in their world. If only adults forgave so freely.

THE POWER OF A PEN AND PAPER

> *A gentle answer turns away wrath, but a harsh word stirs up anger . . . A man finds joy in giving an apt reply—and how good is a timely word! . . . A cheerful look brings joy to the heart, and good news gives health to the bones.*
>
> Proverbs 15:1, 23, 30

Florence Littauer wrote a book entitled *A Letter Is a Gift Forever*. I didn't even need to open the cover to be inspired to write letters to friends and relatives. I felt young again, like in the carefree days of my childhood when I was introduced to real stationery with coordinating stickers. I sent letters to my grandparents and aunties in hopes of a return envelope with *only* my name on the front.

Kids love writing letters; well, at least for a while when they first figure out how to communicate on paper. Several of the most adorable notes that my children scribed are saved for posterity in a clear, plastic shoe box in my closet. They are extracted every once in a lonely while when I need a smile booster. Allow me to share a few of my favorites.

At six, Keeve went through a "dashes" phase where he separated his words with dashes instead of spaces. Corresponding with the dashes was his "Q" phase. We're not quite sure why he wrote a Q after his name, but it lasted for approximately 18 months. One note from that era read, "I-no-you-will-be-happy-bekuse-I-love-you-Mom-from-Keeve-Q." Right he was; I was happy!

Austin is our non-touchy-feely child. He will endure a back rub or a quick hug and kiss, but he's not demonstrative in the least with his emotions. True to his character, his written notes are no-nonsense. At eight years old, his attempt at an affectionate letter brought a huge smile to my face: "Mom, I love you. I will kiss you once. Austin." No "from." No "love." Just "Austin" and one kiss.

One February, when Larisa was five, she wrote a poem for her daddy. Some of it she even made up herself. You guess which part.

Violets are blue.

Roses are red.

On Valentine's Day,

I'm glad you are Dad.

The word *dead* would have fit more poetically, but the true heartfelt meaning would have been lost had she gone with the obvious choice.

Proverbs 15:23 tells us, "A man finds joy in giving an apt reply—and how good is a timely word!" Solomon was right on the money with this slice of wisdom. It is such a simple gesture to jot a little encouraging card to our kids. It takes three minutes, but it can be treasured forever. Make the time to give forever gifts. My grandfather, C.W.T. Chauncey, once wrote, "It is with the greatest of pleasure I grasp this pen with my thumb and finger, and be like a little spider and drop you a line."

WHEN ALL ELSE FAILS, PUT THE YOUNGEST IN CHARGE

> *Be kind and compassionate to one another, forgiving each other just as in Christ God forgave you. Be imitators of God, therefore, as dearly loved children and live a life of love, just as Christ loved us and gave himself up for us as a fragrant offering and sacrifice to God.*
>
> Ephesians 4:32; 5:2

Sibling rivalry was not supposed to happen in our Christ-centered, Ephesians 4:32, "Be-ye-kind" home. I'm not sure when the focus changed from J.O.Y. (Jesus, Others, then You) to M&M (Me and Me), but it did and some intervention was called for.

My middle child was on a self-guided mission to drive his little brother crazy. All the "Stop it!" "Leave me alone!" and "He's bugging me!" were pushing me toward psychosis. I surmised that Austin wasn't getting enough of my attention, so I gave extra love and kisses. Didn't help. Next, I tried separating the boys. No change. Then I made them hug and kiss each other. Nada. Creative discipline used to be my forte, but quite simply, my creative juices had drizzled away along with brotherly kindness. Finally in exasperation, I announced in a less-than-Christ like tone, "If you bug your brother one more time, you will have to do whatever he says for 30 minutes!" I was dead serious. They only snickered.

Five minutes later a smack rang out with a yelp on its heels. Keeve was instructed to come up with some form of punishment for his brother who teased him incessantly. Expected consequences, I assumed, would be sit in the corner, write an apology note, or do his brother's chores. Not so. The victim in this case had carefully calculated the worst possible chastening with his brother's personality and temperament in mind. Six-year-old Keeve pronounced doom: "Run from the front door to the back door in your underwear. Then drink a full glass of tomato juice." Very creative! Those suggestions were *way* outside of the box for my thinking. Inadvertently, a giggle bubbled up inside of me and spilled out.

Austin went into a mild case of shock, his jaw resting on his chest. Austin is extremely modest. Even when heading to take a shower, his clean underwear is stuffed under his shirt so no one would see it. Running in his underwear in broad daylight with an audience mortified him. Keeve could not have picked a worse form of torture for his brother. Bamboo shoots under the fingernails would have been easier for Austin to endure. And tomato juice, well, imagine your most disgusting food . . . and having to consume a large amount of it.

The punishments were carried out, amazingly followed by a month without any sibling rivalry. Thank the good Lord for another boost to my mothering morale.

Squeezing Laughter into a Leotard

> *Do you not know that in a race all the runners run, but only one gets the prize? Run in such a way as to get the prize. Everyone who competes in the games goes into strict training. They do it to get a crown that will not last; but we do it to get a crown that will last forever.*
>
> 1 Corinthians 9:24,25

Some "brainiac" spent valuable mental processing time figuring out that "desserts" spelled backwards is "stressed." What in the world, pray tell, does that mean? If I'm stressed I simply need a dessert to take off the edge? Or is it that desserts cause stress? You want stress? Look at the multiple pages in restaurant menus listing sugar laden, fat-cementing-on-my-thighs, gooey foods of the gods.

Eating healthily intrigues me. Quite frankly, sugar intrigues me. Regularly exercising intrigues me. Squeezing into leotards intrigues me too. Leotards spelled backwards should be "stressed", but it's not. It's "sdratoel." For far too many years I blamed my double-wide behind on "baby fat," as if it were glued on after I delivered each child. I resisted leotards and wheat grass.

One frightening day I passed an overweight woman in a department store. I didn't pay her much attention, as I was focused on my immediate shopping need. Instantaneously (actually it was after a full two-second delay), I jolted to a halt, realizing that what I had passed was a mirror. Mirror spelled backwards should be a swear word in my books.

An announcement was made that night that a leotard plan was commencing at sunrise. Onto the blasted treadmill I climbed at O'dark thirty. Running does not intrigue me, unless I'm being chased. With the vision of the department store lady in my mind, I began one of several uphill-all-the-way, get-me-back-into-shape regimens.

Over and over, I quoted my high school's theme verse: "But they that wait upon the Lord shall renew their strength; they shall mount up with wings as eagles, they shall run, and not be weary: and they shall walk, and not faint" (Isaiah 40:31). Mental toughness was building. I could sense it.

Right when I was feeling good about my exercising feat, from behind the treadmill, I heard one of my baby-fat-causing-chicks utter these unthinkable words: "Hey, you guys, come here and watch Mom's bum wiggle." As if there was free popcorn and cotton candy, they all came . . . and enjoyed the show. The evil eagle in me yearned to let go of the treadmill bar, land on the eaglets and wring their scrawny, little featherless necks. Yet, on I treaded, resisting temptation.

Forgive me, Lord, for not taking better care of myself, and for momentarily plotting to hurt my sweet children. Being in the "hindsight" position probably was humorous. Please restore the laughter in my heart. Amen.